JN411757

미서부 & 밴쿠버 여행

By Servas

미 서부 & 밴쿠버 여행 By Servas

니도 가고 싶나? 세계 평화 무료 민박 여행

초판 1쇄 발행 2025년 12월 31일

지은이 김효정
펴낸이 장길수
펴낸곳 지식과감성#
출판등록 제2012-000081호

교정 주경민
디자인 이현
편집 이현
검수 이주연
마케팅 김윤길

주소 서울시 금천구 벚꽃로298 대륭포스트타워6차 1212호
전화 070-4651-3730~4
팩스 070-4325-7006
이메일 ksbookup@naver.com
홈페이지 www.knsbookup.com

ISBN 979-11-392-3014-7(03810)
값 20,000원

지식과감성#
홈페이지 바로가기

미서부 & 밴쿠버 여행 By Servas

글, 그림, 사진 김효정

니도 가고 싶나?
세계 평화 무료 민박 여행

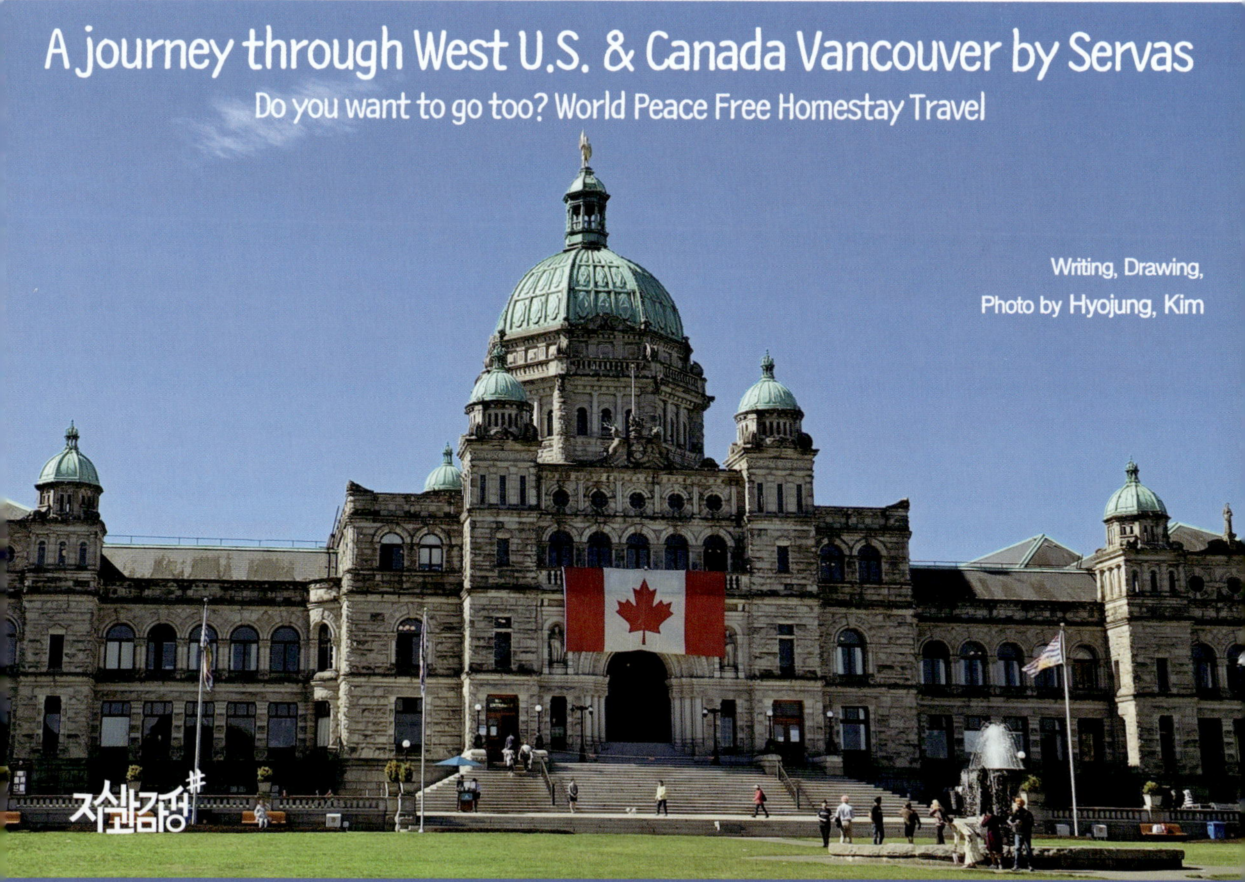

서문

서바스를 통해 세계 곳곳을 여행한다. 머무는 집마다 한국 선물을 가져가서 우리나라 음식과 노래, 관광지 등을 소개한다. 두 번이나 머문 노르웨이의 아시(Asborg) 언니가 몇 해 전에 출판된 내 책을 읽고 싶다고 하여 책 내용 몇 페이지를 번역하여 보내준 적이 있었다.

이번에 방문했던 펄루스 밀밭은 미국 호스트 가족들도 가보지 못한 곳이라 하였다. 내가 다녔던 소도시에서 느꼈던 감정과 숨어있는 미국과 밴쿠버 곳곳을 소개하고 싶어서 여행기를 썼다. 영어로 번역해서 호스트에게 선물하고 싶은 마음이 컸다.

혼자 번역하다가 힘들어서 구글과 네이버 번역 사이트를 비교하며 활용하였다. 애매한 것은 통번역 자격증을 가진 딸의 도움을 받았다. 한글이 얼마나 풍부한 어휘를 가진 창의적인 문자인지 다시금 느꼈다. 형용사 표현과, 은유법 표현, 내가 느낀 생각과 감정을 그대로 번역할 수 없어 안타깝고 아쉬웠다. 마지막 단계에, 내가 머물렀던 호스트에게 잘못된 내용이나 문법 등을 고쳐달라고 부탁하였다. 그들이 사용하는 단어와 문장으로 나의 글을 자세하게 고쳐준 호스트와 내가 근무했던 학교의 원어민 교사 션에게 진심으로 고마움을 전한다.

나를 편안하게 대해주고, 정성껏 요리해 준 서바스 회원들이 가족처럼 느껴진다. 독립된 숙소를 제공한 에밀리 가족, 한국에 대해 열심히 공부하고 내 글을 잘 고쳐준 앤과 데이브, 한국 며느리를 가진 다재다능한 린과 존, 밤 산책을 함께 해준 바바라 가족, 바쁜 일정에도 호스트 해준 수잔과 키트, 아주 세세하게 문장을 체크해 주신 존과 모니카에게 진심으로 감사와 존경을 드린다.

항상 나를 응원해 주는 우리 가족, 함께 여행한 서바스 후배님, 짧은 기간에 책을 완성시켜 준 지식과감성# 출판사 가족에게도 고마움을 전한다.

뻔한 미국 여행에서 벗어나 소도시에 관심을 가지는 여행을 좋아하는 독자에게 도움이 되는 책이길 바란다.

2025년 겨울의 길목에서

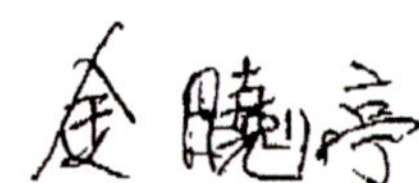

PROLOGUE

I travel the world through Servas. I bring Korean gifts to every home I stay in, introducing them to Korean food, music, and tourist attractions. A Norwegian woman Asborg, whom I've visited twice, once said she wanted to read a book I published a few years ago, so I translated a few pages and sent them to her.

This time, I visited the Palouse Wheat Fields were a place even my American host family hadn't been to. I wrote a travelogue to share the emotions I felt in the small towns I visited and to share the hidden gems of the United States and Vancouver. I also had a strong desire to translate it into English and give it to my hosts as a gift.

It was difficult to translate by myself, so I compared and utilized translation sites like Google and Naver. Things I was unsure of were helped by my daughter, a certified interpreter and translator. I felt again how rich and creative Korean is with its vocabulary. It was a pity and disappointment that I could not translate adjective expressions, metaphors, and the thoughts and feelings I felt. In the final step, I asked my host to correct any wrong information or grammatical errors in my writing. I sincerely thanks all the hosts for correcting my writing in detail with the words and sentences they use and Sean, a native-speaking teacher at the school where I worked.

The Servas members who treated me comfortably and cooked with care feel like family. I would like to express my sincere gratitude and respect to Emily's family for providing independent accommodations, Ann and Dave for their diligent study of Korea and their insightful comments, the versatile Lynn and John with their Korean daughter-in-law, Barbara's family taking a night walks, Suzanne and Kit for their hosting despite their busy schedules, and John and Monica for their meticulously checked sentences.

I would also like to express my gratitude to my family who always supports me, my junior Servas who traveled with me, and the Knowledge and Emotion publishing family who helped me complete the book in a short period of time.

I hope this book will be helpful to readers who enjoy traveling and are interested in small towns and escape the typical American travel itinerary.

at the crossroads of winter Hyojung Kim(MAY)

차례

여행 계획과 서바스 소개

시애틀

올림픽 반도

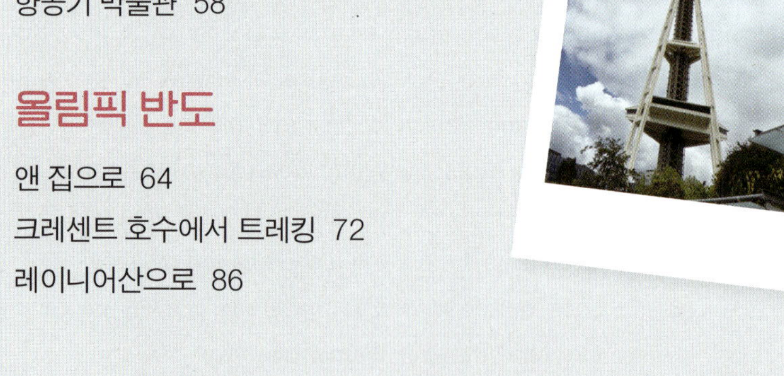

Table of Contents

포틀랜드

펄루스

PART 6

우드번

Portland

Palouse

Woodburn

PART 7 다시 시애틀로

PART 8 밴쿠버 아일랜드

PART 9 밴쿠버

Back to Seattle

Vancouver Island

Vancouver

여행 계획과 서바스 소개

시애틀-밴쿠버 여행 (2025. 5. 14. ~ 2025. 6. 3. 20박 21일)

날짜	출발	도착	숙소/연락처		볼거리	맛집, 기타
5/14 (수)	Jeju 7C112 (11:15)	GMP (12:30)	Emily	14	Fremont Troll, Amazone Spheres, 워싱턴 대학, 스카이뷰 전망대(티켓), 컬럼비아 센터	제주항공-대한항공
	인천 KE41 (16:40)	시애틀 (10:40)		15	스타벅스 1호, 퍼블릭 마켓, Pier 66, 껌벽, 스페이스니들(티켓), Chihuly Garden Glass Museum, Kerry park(야경뷰), Lake union, 시애틀 공립 도서관	Laurie 206 371 1003 전화하기
				16	비행기 박물관(티켓)	렌터카 빌리기.
5/16 (금)		Port Angeles	Ann	16	Lake Crescent Lodge, Forks(트와일라잇 배경) 마을	
				17	https://www.nps.gov/olym/planyourvisit/day-hiking-at-olympic.htm Olympic National Park(티켓) Rialto Beach Quinault valley	입장료 자동차, 사람 함께 구입하기
5/18 (일)		Portland	Lynn / John	18	Mount Ranier N.P 거쳐서 Cannon Beach 일몰 찍고 호스트네로	
				19	다운타운	
				20	폭포 탐방	폭포 2~3곳 고르기
5/21 (수)		Colfax Amy- 에어비앤비 숙소 예약(3박) Head east out of Colfax on 272 heading towards Palouse for 1 mile then take a left onto Hilty Road go out 2.2 miles. We are located on the left hand side of the road.		21 수	Palouse	숙소 $89.11(4/8 선금결제) $356.41(5/21 결재) 밀밭 사진 찍기 Colfax, Pullman, Moscow 시내 나들이
				22 목	Steptoe Butte-Palouse Hill, Palouse Falls	
				23 금	Kamiak Butte	
		좋으면 같은 숙소 연장 안 좋으면 다른 곳으로 이동		24 토	snake river canyeon(숙소에서 3:40 거리)	
5/25 (일)		Barbara		25 일	Leavenworth-독일 마을/Minchen Haus 핫도그 Snoqualmie Fall, 시애틀 아울렛	
5/26 (월)				26	시애틀 못 가본 곳 가기	
5/27 (화)		빅토리아	Suzanne	27	시애틀-밴쿠버(버스비) 밴쿠버-빅토리아섬(지하철비와 배 삯)	렌터카 반납
				28	국회의사당, 크레이그다로치 성, 부차드가든(티켓), Royal BC Museum	렌터카 빌리기.
				29	섬 드라이브	
5/30 (금)		밴쿠버	Monica / John	30	섬-밴쿠버(지하철비와 뱃삯), UBC 대학	
				31	잉글리시 베이, 그랜빌 아일랜드, 스탠리 공원, 개스타운, 캐나다 플레이스, 퀸 엘리자베스 공원	
				1	캐필라노 서스펜스 다리, 시해벤섬, 스쿼미시, 휘슬러-렌터카 하면	
				2	아침 시간 어딘가 들러보든지, 12시까지 공항 가기	
6/2	밴쿠버 KE72 (14:50)	6/3 인천 (17:50)				아시아나항공
6/3	김포 아시아나 (21:00)	제주 (22:00)				

▶ 개인 준비물

입국서 : 비행기에서 받아서 쓰기

여권, 비자(ESTA), 항공권 출력, 현금 약간, 트래블카드(미리 만들어서 달러 약간 입금 해놓기), 해외 사용 카드

전기 110V용 어댑터, 유심(E심- 갤럭시 S23 가능/ Verizon 미국, 캐나다 가능) / 옷 밴쿠버는 조금 더 쌀쌀함/ 시애틀은 5월이면 낮에는 20도 정도

1)여름 티셔츠, 얇은 바지 2)춘추용 긴팔과 바지 3)얇은 패딩 4)바람막이 점퍼 5)모자 여러 개 6)스카프 여러 개

7)마스크 8)속옷과 양말 9)운동화/편한 신발 10)사랄라 원피스나 스커트 - 사진 찍을 때 쓸 수 있으니 11)화장품, 복용약/소화제, 연고, 세면도구/폼클렌징/팩

기타: 우산, 보온병(500ml 이상), 동전지갑, 메모지, 물티슈, 선글라스, 지퍼팩 대/중/먹거리: 컵라면 2개(이동 시), 햇반 2개

선물 준비 후배(와인 커버 6, 수저세트 6, 파우치 8) 음식: 청정원 불고기 양념 2개(2.4kg용), 오뚜기 자른 당면 1개(20인용)

나 준비(손녀 한복, 전통 태극 부채, 제주 지도 손수건, 전통 액자 2개, 열쇠고리 등) 음식: 제주 과자, 사탕, 마른 미역

Travel Planning and Introduction to Servas

봄날의 여행과 서바스 소개

그동안 나의 해외여행은 비록 그 시간이 짧을지라도 사람을 만나는 것에 우선을 두었다. 이번 여행은 펄루스(Palouse) 지역의 밀밭을 카메라에 담고 싶다는 계획이 먼저였다. 인터넷에 게시된 밀밭 풍광이 뇌리에 꽂혀서 손꼽을 버킷리스트가 되었다. 꼭 한번 가리라 마음먹었는데 동행할 서바스(Servas) 후배가 생겨서 빨리 실행에 옮길 수 있었다.

서바스는 2차 세계전쟁 후 전쟁의 참상을 느낀 미국인 밥 루이트바일러(Bob Luitweiler)와 그의 유럽 친구들이 전쟁을 반대하는 피스 빌더스(Peace builders)라는 운동으로 시작되었다.

1949년 덴마크에서 태동한 서바스는 인간의 존엄성과 신뢰를 바탕으로, 평화로운 세상 만들기를 장기 목표로 두는 세계평화 민박 단체이다. 종교와 언어, 인종과 민족을 초월하여 사람들이 만나서 소통하고, 생각과 문화를 공유하면서 사람과 지구 환경을 돌보는 것에 가치를 둔다.

1952년 처음 세계 모임 때 서바스(Servas)라 이름 붙였다. 서바스는 19세기에 세계 공용어였던 에스페란토 언어로 'We Serve', 즉 봉사를 뜻한다.

1972년 스위스 등기소에 등록하고, 세계 서바스가 정식으로 출범하였다. 다른 지역에서 3년마다 세계 총회를 개최하며, 지구 환경과 세계평화에 관심을 가진다. 현재 유엔 경제사회이사회 비정부기구(NGO) 협의, 유엔여성위원회 회의에서도 활약 중이다.

Spring Travel and Introducing Servas

In the meantime, my overseas trips, even if the time was short, prioritized meeting people, This trip was initially planned to capture the wheat fields of the Palouse area on camera. The wheat field scenery posted on the internet stuck in my mind, and it became a bucket list item. I was determined to go there at least once, and thanks to my junior, Servas, joining me, so I was able to quickly put it into action.

Servas was started by American Bob Luitweiler and his European friends as a movement called Peace Builders, who felt the horrors of war after World War II and opposed war.

Founded in Denmark in 1949, Servas is a world peace homestay organization with a long-term goal of creating a peaceful world based on human dignity and trust. It values people to meet and communicate beyond religion, language, race and ethnicity, sharing idea and culture, and caring for people and the global environment.

It was named "Servas" at the first world meeting in 1952. Servas means "We Serve" in Esperanto, the world's official language in the 19th century.

It was registered with the Swiss Registery in 1972, and the Servas International was officially launched. The world assembly meeting held in a different region every three years and concerned with global environment and world peace. Currently, the Servas is active in the UN Economic and Social Council NGO Consultations and the UN Women's Committee Meeting.

우리나라는 1965년 부산에서 의사였던 고(故) 이병훈 박사에 의해 소개되었다. 1976년에 한국서바스 첫 총회를 개최하고 활동하다가 이 박사가 일본으로 거주지를 옮기면서 공백이 생겼다. 고(故) 임재량 고문이 1986년에 이탈리아 세계 총회에 참가하여 세계 총회 투표권을 얻었다. 1989년에 한국서바스 회장으로서 이 박사에게서 서바스를 인계받아 발전시켰다.

한국서바스 회원들은 동아세안 회의, 아프리카 회의, 세계 총회 등에 참여하였다. 2018년에 서울에서 개최된 세계 총회에 53개국 165명의 회원이 참가하여 성황리에 마쳤다. 현재 세계 회원국은 100개가 넘었고, 한국에는 11개 지부에 약 230여 명의 회원이 활동 중이다.

회원 가입은 지인 소개나 홈페이지를 통해서 할 수 있다. 그 후, 자신이 거주하는 지역장과 인터뷰를 거쳐서 통과하면, 약간의 가입비와 연회비를 내고 회원이 된다. 여행 시에는 회원 인증 스탬프(Letter of Information) 비용을 낸다. 우리가 가고자 하는 곳의 호스트에게 메일을 보내고, 그들이 수락하면 머물 수 있다.

보통 2~3일 머물지만 호스트가 허락하면 더 머물 수도 있다. 서바스 규칙으로는 숙소만 제공해도 괜찮으나 숟가락 하나 더 얹는다는 마음으로 첫날은 호스트가 저녁을 준비한다. 둘째 날은 게스트가 저녁을 대접하는데, 내 경우는 현지에서 음식 재료를 사고, 한국에서 준비해 간 소스로 불고기, 김밥, 잡채, 미역국이나 전 등을 요리하였다.

Korean Servas was introduced in 1965 by the late Lee Byung-hoon, who was a doctor in Busan. In 1976, the first general meeting of the Korean Servas was held and active, but Dr. Lee moved his residence to Japan, creating a gap. Lim Jae-ryang, the late advisor, participated in the Italian International Meeting in 1986 to gain the right to vote for the World Assembly. As the chairman of the Servas Korea in 1989, he took over from Dr. Lee and developed it.

After that, members participated in the East Asian Conference, the African Conference, and the International General Assembly. In 2018, the SICOGA(Servas International Conference and General Assembly) was held in Seoul and successfully concluded with 165 members from 53 countries participating. Currently, there are more than 100 member states of the world, and about 230 members are active in 11 branches in Korea.

You can sign up for membership through a friend's introduction or through the website. After that, if you pass the interview with the local head of the area you live in, you can become a member by paying a small membership fee and annual fee. When traveling, you pay for membership verification(Letter of Information) stamp. Send an email to the host where we want to go, and we can stay if they accept.

We usually stay for two or three days, but we can stay more if the host allows us. Host only provide accommodation, but on the first day, the host cooks dinner with the mind of putting one more spoon on top. The next day, the guest treated the host to dinner, and in my case, I bought ingredients locally and cooked bulgogi, kimbap, japchae, seaweed soup or Korean style pancakes with sauce I had prepared in Korea.

2014년 서바스 회원이 된 나는 2015년 처음으로 폴란드 회원을 호스트하였고, 이어서 여러 나라에서 온 회원들을 호스트하였다. 해외여행 시, 2016년 동유럽을 시작으로 유럽의 여러 나라, 호주, 심지어 모로코 서바스 회원 댁에 머물렀다. 긴 여행에서 항공료보다 많이 지출되는 숙박비를 절약할 수 있는 것이 큰 장점이다.

시기에 따라 다르지만 항공권은 보통 6개월 전에 예약하면 저렴하게 살 수 있다. 하루 전에 아주 싸게 파는 땡처리 항공권이 나오기도 하지만 한 번도 이용한 적은 없었다. 5월에 출발했던 항공권은 1월에 예약하였다.

현지인 집에서 생활하며 그들 문화를 접하고, 생각을 공유한다. 짧은 기간이지만 밥을 함께 먹는 식구가 되어 그들 삶에 스며들었다. 시애틀부터 밴쿠버까지 3주 동안 머물렀던 여섯 호스트에게 수저 2세트, 한복 와인 커버, 누비 파우치, 태극부채, 제주 지도가 그려진 스카프 등 다섯 가지 공통 선물을 드렸다. 한국 기념품을 드리고, 한국 음식을 대접하며 우리나라 풍습과 문화를 소개하는 등 민간외교관 역할을 하였다. 좋은 사람과의 만남을 통해 행복하고 즐거운 여행이 되었다.

After becoming a Servas member in 2014, I hosted a Polish member for the first time in 2015, followed by members from various countries. When traveling abroad, I stayed at Servas's homes in several European countries, Australia, and even Morocco, starting with Eastern Europe in 2016. The big advantage is that you can save on accommodation costs that are more expensive than airfare on long trips.

It depends on the season, you can usually get cheaper airfare if you book six months in advance. There are times when a very cheap flight ticket is sold the day before, but I have never used it. The flight departing in May was booked in January.

I stay at Servas host home, come into contact with their culture, and share my thoughts. Although it was a short period of time, I became a family that ate with them and permeated their lives. We gave five common gifts to the six hosts who stayed for three weeks from Seattle to Vancouver: two sets of cutlery, a hanbok wine cover, a quilted pouch, a Taegeuk fan, and a scarf with a Jeju map on it, I acted as private diplomat, giving out Korean souvenirs as gifts, cooking Korean food, and introducing our country's customs and culture. It was a happy and enjoyable trip through meeting a good person.

사전에 가족 수나 취향 등을 파악하여 호스트 가족에게 어울릴 만한 특별한 선물을 내가 따로 챙겨 갔다. 한복, 전통 혼인 모습이 담긴 액자, 직접 만든 액세서리, 지갑, 무릎 담요 등을 가져갔다. 작은 선물에도 감사하는 그들의 모습을 보니 나 역시 행복해졌다.

여행 경험을 공유하고, K 문화의 현상을 비롯하여 세상 사는 이야기를 나누었다. 어떤 가족은 한국 문화에 무척 관심이 많아서 K 드라마를 같이 보기도 하였다.

짧은 시간이지만 같이 생활하고 이야기를 나누다 보면 자연스럽게 친해진다. 귀국 후에도 계속 연락하고, 특별한 날에 선물을 보내고, 해마다 크리스마스카드나 새해 연하장을 보냈다. 답장으로 엽서나 카드를 보내주는 회원도 있었고, 메일이나 문자 또는 전화를 하기도 하였다.

회원을 넘어 친구가 되고, 더 친해지면 글로벌 가족이 되어 자연스럽게 시스터(Sister)라 부른다. 친구가 된 헬싱키 오티(Outi), 언니가 된 스타방에르 아시(Asborg) 댁에는 두 번씩 다녀오기도 하였다.

우리 집에 머물렀던 네덜란드, 스페인, 이스라엘, 프랑스 회원 댁을 내가 방문하였고, 반대로 내가 머물렀던 대만 회원은 내가 제주에 살 때 우리집에 방문하였다. 한국의 품앗이 풍습처럼 서바스는 서로 왕래가 가능한 시스템을 가지고 있다.

옷깃만 스쳐도 인연인데 같이 밥을 먹고, 대화를 나누며 생각을 공유하고, 한 공간에서 잠을 자는 생활은 얼마나 깊은 인연일까. 인연을 선연(善緣)으로 이어간다.

I took special gifts that would suit my host family by finding out their family members and preferences in advance. I brought hanbok, a picture frame with a traditional weeding scene, handmade accessories, a wallet, and lap blanket. I was also happy to see they appreciate even a small gift.

We shared travel experiences and talked about living in the world, including the phenomenon of K culture. Some families were so interested in Korean culture that we watched K-drama together.

Even though it's a short time, we live together and talk, we will naturally become close. I kept in touch even after returning home, sent gifts on special days, and sent Christmas cards or New Year's cards every year. Some host sent postcards or cards as replies, while others sent emailed, texted, or phoned.

Beyond being members, we become friends, and as we become closer, we become a global family and naturally call each other "sisters." I visited twice both of them; Helsinki Outi, who became friends, and Stavanger Asborg, who became an older sister.

I visited the homes of the Dutch, Spanish, Israeli, and French members who stayed at my house, and conversely, I visited the homes of the Taiwanese members who stayed at my house when I was living in Jeju. Similar to Korea's 'Pumasi' tradition, Servas is based on a reciprocal system that allows members to both host and guest.

They say that even a passing encounter is still a connection, how much deeper it be to share a meal, converse, share thoughts, and sleep in same space? This connection leads to good relationship.

민족과 인종을 초월하여, 종교와 언어의 벽을 뛰어넘는 문화 확산과 IT 기술로 점점 지구촌이 가까워졌다. 반면에 제 민족, 자기 국가만을 우등 국가라 생각하는 엉터리 지도자 때문에 전쟁의 도가니에 빠져서 많은 사람이 죽고, 고통을 받고 있다.

서바스는 평화로운 세상을 만드는 작은 씨앗의 역할을 톡톡히 한다. 전혀 모르는 낯선 이의 방문을 의심하지 않고 환영한다. 대가를 바라지 않고 정성을 다해 대접하며, 사랑과 이해로 지구촌 가족을 만들면서 세계평화에 이바지한다.

The spread of culture and IT technology, transcending nationality, race, religion, and language barriers, have brought the world close together. On the other hand, many people are dying and suffering in the crucible of war because of a foolish leader who thinks only his own people and country are superior.

Servas plays a vital role of a small seed that creates a peaceful world. We welcome complete strangers without suspicion. We serve with all our heart without expecting a price, and contribute to world peace by creating a global family with love and understanding.

시애틀

Seattle

호스트
에밀리 집으로

펄루스를 가기 위해 시애틀을 기점으로 삼았다. 14일 15시, 인천에서 국적기로 출발하니 마음이 편했다. 마음먹기에 따라서 못 할 것이 없는 게 인간의 무한한 가능성인 듯하다. 시차 적응을 위해 11시간 동안 기내에서 한숨도 자지 않았다. 영화를 보고, 음악을 들으며 견뎠다. 태평양을 건너 날아왔는데도 시애틀 타코마 공항에 도착한 시각은 14일 10시경이었다. 덤으로 하루를 벌었다는 생각에 왠지 기분이 좋았다.

시애틀에는 두 번째 방문이었다. 다문화교육 박사과정 중 워싱턴 주립대학의 뱅크스(Banks J. A.) 교수 연구소에 방문하기 위해서 2014년에 방문하였다. 그때 머물렀던 에어비앤비 숙소, 에티오피아 출신 주인 할머니의 친절 때문에 시애틀은 좋은 추억으로 남아있던 곳이다.

국력의 척도는 정치, 경제, 문화, 군사, 외교 등이 일반적이다. 2014년 미국 방문 시에는 검사원이 나를 무시하는 눈초리로 엄격하게 검사를 하였다. 반면 이번에는 출입국 관리소에서 친절하게 대해주며 빠르게 통과시켜 주었다. K 문화 확산으로 국력이 무척 성장했음을 실감하였다.

공항 로비가 무척 인상적이었다. 짐을 찾으러 내려가는 곳에 구겨진 스카프 모양의 긴 구조물이 몇 군데나 설치되어 있었다. 잊지 말고 아울렛 매장에 들러 소비하고 가라는 의도였겠지만 관광객의 눈을 멈추게 하는 멋진 광고판과 다름없었다.

Go to Host Emily's house

I set Seattle as my starting point to go to Palouse. At 3 p.m. on the 14th, I felt relieved as I departed from Incheon with KAL. It seems that human potential is infinite, that there is nothing we cannot do if we put our minds to it. I didn't sleep even a wink on the plane for 11 hours to adjust to the jet lag. I endured it while watching movies and listening to music. Even though I flew across the Pacific Ocean, I arrived at Seattle's Tacoma Airport around 10 a.m. on the 14th. I felt good thinking that I made a day off on bonuses.

It was my second visit to Seattle. In 2014, I visited University of Washington's reserch institute of James A. Banks. During my doctoral course in multicultural education, Seattle remained a good memory because of the kindness of Ethiopian grandmother who was the owner of the Airbnb accommodation.

Politics, economy, culture, military, and diplomacy are common measures of national power. When visiting the United States in 2014, the inspectors ignored me and were strictly examined. On the other hand, this time, the immigration office treated me kindly and let me pass quickly. I realized that Korea's national power has grown a lot due to the spread of K culture.

The airport lobby was very impressive. Several crumpled scarf-shaped long structures were installed at the way down to pick up my luggage. Although the intention was to stop by the outlet store for consumption, it was fancy billboard that caught the attention of tourists.

호스트 에밀리(Emily)네로 가기 위해 우선 링크(Link)라는 전철을 타야 했다. 어디든지 처음은 낯설다. 전철 티켓을 어떻게 사는지 몰라 머뭇거리고 있으니 봉사하고 계신 노신사께서 친절하게 알려주었다.

편하게 쉬실 나이임에도 불구하고 웃는 모습으로 봉사하는 태도에 나도 덩달아 미소가 번졌다. 용돈벌이인지, 보람된 시간을 갖기 위함인지 모르겠으나 어릴 적부터 봉사가 몸에 밴 분이라 생각하니 저절로 고개가 숙여졌다.

카드를 먼저 사고, 후에 다시 일정액을 충전하는 방법이 나라마다 비슷했다. 전철 타고, 버스로 갈아타고, 다시 걸어서 집으로 향했다.

호주나 미국은 도시를 만들 때 가장 먼저 도로를 확보하고 학교, 관공서, 주택지 등을 마련한다. 도로 이름에다 홀수와 짝수로 붙여서 주소를 만들기 때문에 집 찾기가 어렵지 않다.

버스에서 내려 큰 도로를 따라 걷다가 작은 도로로 들어섰다. 양쪽으로 마주한 홀수, 짝수 주소를 가진 집들은 제각각 건축 양식이 달랐다. 건축 공부하는 사람이 유럽으로만 탐방하지 말고 미국으로 와도 배움의 장소가 되겠다. 외관이 똑같은 집은 하나도 없다. 땅 모양이 크든 작든 집 앞뜰에는 다양한 봄꽃이 피어 길을 걷는 사람을 행복하게 만들기에 충분하였다. 길거리 공원이라 이름 붙여도 좋겠다.

In order to get to the host Emily's house, I had to take the subway called Link first. It is strange for me to go anywhere for the first time. I was hesitating not knowing how to buy a subway ticket, so an old gentleman who was volunteering kindly informed me.

Even though the gentleman was old enough to rest comfortably, I also smiled at his attitude of serving with a smile. I don't know if he's making pocket money or serving to have a rewarding time, but thinking that had learned since childhood naturally made me respect him.

The method of buying a card first and then charging a certain amount again was similar in each country. I took the subway, changed to a bus, and walked back home.

Australia or the United States are the first to secure roads and prepare schools, government offices, and residential areas when creating cities. It is not difficult to find a house because the address is made by attaching odd and even numbers to the name of the road.

After getting off the bus, I walked along the main road and entered the small road. Houses with odd or even addresses facing each other on both sides had different architectural styles. It will be a place for architecture learners to learn even if they come to the United States instead of exploring Europe. No house has the same appearance. Whether the land is large or small, various spring flowers bloom in the front yard of the house, making people happy. It would be nice to name it a street park.

에밀리네 앞뜰에 핀 이름 모를 꽃들이 우리를 반겨주었다. 에밀리는 우리를 뒤뜰로 안내하였다. 몇 마리의 닭이 닭장에서 낯선 우리를 쳐다보았다. 작은 텃밭에는 시금치, 상추, 파 등 익숙한 푸성귀가 자라고 있었다. 토양이 좋은지 우리나라 채소보다 훨씬 컸다. 시애틀은 생활비와 물가가 비싸서 텃밭에서 채소를 가꾸는 집이 많다고 하였다.

다섯 가족이 함께 사는 3층 집, 어느 방에서 머물지 은근히 기대했는데, 호스트를 위한 모든 것을 갖춘 뒤뜰 독채에 머물러야 했다. 후배와 둘만 생활하는 공간이라 불편한 점은 없었지만 뭔가 아쉽고 씁쓸하였다. 에밀리가 준비한 웰컴 티(Welcome tea)와 빵으로 간단하게 점심을 먹고, 시애틀 관광 정보를 얻은 후, 길을 나섰다.

The unnamed flowers in Emily's front yard welcomed us. She led us to the backyard. Several chickens looked at the strangers in the henhouse. In the small garden, familiar vegetables such as spinach, lettuce, and green onions were growing. Maybe the soil was good, so the vegetables were much bigger than those in our country. Emily told me that Seattle has high cost of living, so there are many houses that grow vegetables in the garden.

I was secretly looking forward to a three-story house where five families live together, which room I would stay in, but I had to stay in a backyard detached house with everything for the host. There was nothing uncomfortable about living with my junior, but I felt something was unfortunate and bitter. I went out after getting Seattle tourism information over lunch with a welcome tea and bread prepared by Emily.

스페이스 니들

스페이스 니들은 시애틀의 랜드마크다. 1962년 세계 박람회를 위해 만들어진 것으로 당시에는 미국 내에서 가장 높았던 180m 빌딩이다. 과학 전시장에서나 볼 수 있는 UFO를 연상시키는 외관이 우주를 탐험하고자 하는 인간의 마음을 고스란히 담은 건축물로 주목받았다.

엘리베이터를 타러 가는 길에는 스페이스 니들 건축 역사에 대한 사진과 설명이 있었다. 1962년, 우리나라는 전쟁 후 여러모로 불안정한 상황에서 경제개발 5개년을 시작하며 성장을 위한 발돋움을 한 해이다. 한 치 앞도 내다볼 수 없는 우리로서는 상상조차 하지 못한 일이었다. 미국은 그 시기에 우주를 향한 연구를 시도하였다니 그저 놀라울 따름이었다.

승강기를 이용해서 꼭대기에 오르면 막힘없는 전경에 또 한 번 놀랐다. 마천루 라인이 저만치 발아래 있으니 신선놀음이 아니고 무엇이랴. 꼭대기 층은 회전 유리 바닥이라 가만히 서 있어도 360도의 각기 다른 풍광을 즐길 수 있었다. 벽처럼 설치된 유리에 기대어 바라보는 하늘마저 내 것인 양 한참을 머물렀다. 더 높이 오르려는 인간의 욕심이 나라마다 자꾸 고층 건물을 쏟아내도록 만들었다.

한 층 아래로 내려가면 땅이 보이는 유리 바닥으로 된 공간 위쪽에 자동카메라가 설치된 곳이 있었다. 다양한 포즈를 취하며 인생 숏을 남겼다.

Space Needle

Space Needle is a landmark of Seattle. Built for the 1962 World's Fair, it was the highest 180m building in the United States at the time. The exterior reminiscent of UFOs, which can only be seen in science exhibition halls, has attracted attention as an architecture that contains the human mind to explore space.

On the way to the elevator, there were photos and explanations of the history of the constructing the Space Needle. In 1962, Korea started five years of economic development in a situation of instability after the war in many ways, and it was a year to rise for growth. It would have been unimaginable for us who could not even imagine it. It was just surprising that the United States tried to study space at that time.

When I used the elevator to reach the top, I was once again surprised by the unblocked panoramic view. The skyscraper line was so far below my feet, what else I could were nothing short of god. The top floor was a rotating glass floor, so I could enjoy different 360-degree views even if I stood still. I stayed for a long time, as if the sky I looked at against the wall-mounted glass was mine. Human greed to climb high has led to the continued construction of high-rise buildings in each country.

Down one floor, there was an automatic camera installed above the glass floor space where you could see the ground. I took various poses and left a life shot.

치훌리 유리 정원

스페이스 니들과 치훌리 유리 정원 두 곳의 콤보 티켓을 싸게 산 덕분에 몇 발자국 떨어지지 않은 치훌리 유리 정원(Chihuly Glass Garden)으로 향했다.

첫 번째 방에 들어가니 정면 공간 벽면에는 여러 가지 모양과 색을 가진 양탄자를 연상시키는 많은 천이 길게 늘어뜨린 채 전시되어 있었다. 불빛을 받은 화려한 조각조각의 천들이 밖으로 튀어나올 것만 같았다.

Chihuly Glass Garden

Combo tickets for two places, the Space Needle and the Chihuly Glass Garden, were cheap. I headed to the Chihuly Glass Garden, a few steps from the Space Needle.

When I entered the first room, many fabrics reminiscent of rugs of various shapes and colors were displayed on the wall of the front space. The dazzling, light-struck pieces of fabric looked like they were about to spill out.

이보다 더 화려할 수 있을까. 또 다른 방에서 만난 유리 작품들은 천상계에서나 접할 듯한 화려한 색의 극치를 보여주었다.

바다 생물을 소재로 한 작품을 통해 작가가 바닷가에서 자랐음을 짐작할 수 있었다. 발레리나가 춤을 추듯 말미잘 같은 조각품은 파도에 일렁이며 곧 내 손에 닿을 촉수를 뻗는 듯하였다. 물속을 유영하는 해파리의 유연함은 빛을 받아서 미묘한 색감 변화를 보여주었다. 문어 다리 하나하나의 디테일과 입을 벌린 다양한 조개 모습 등 전시실이 온통 바다 내음으로 넘쳤다. 각각의 유리 공예 작품은 보는 사람마다 다르게 해석할 수 있는 신비로움과 경이로움의 극치였다.

불빛을 받은 유리는 자기가 품은 색보다 더 오묘한 색깔로 빛을 내었다. 작가의 열정과 혼이 고스란히 담긴 유리 작품은 빛과 만나 어떤 재료로도 흉내 내지 못할 훌륭한 예술품으로 탄생하였다.

촉수를 날름거리는 곤충일까, 막 벌어진 꽃봉오리일까? 복도 천정에서 사람들의 눈길을 끌었다. 유리로 만들어진 넓은 공간에도 해파리인지 연꽃인지 모를 붉은 계열의 유리 꽃이 가득 피어 즐거운 에너지를 뿜어내고 있었다.

Could it get any more splendid than this? The glass works I met in another room displayed the extremes of brilliant color that only seemed to come from the heavenly realm.

Through works based on sea creatures, it was possible to guess that the artist grew up on the beach. Just as a ballerina danced, the sculpture like an anemones swayed in the wave, their tentacles reaching out as though they might almost touch my hand. The jellyfish's flexibility in the water received light and showed subtle color changes. The exhibition room was full of the smell of the sea, including the details of each octopus leg and the appearance of various clams with their mouths open. Each glass craft was the height of mystery and wonder that could be interpreted differently by each viewer.

The glass that received the light glowed with a more subtle color than its own. Glass works containing the artist's passion and soul were created as excellent artworks that could not be imitated by any material when they met light.

Is it an insect that flies its tentacles or a bud that just opened? It caught people's attention from the ceiling of the hallway. Even in a large space made of glass, red glass flowers, which were either jellyfish or lotus flowers, were in full bloom, radiating joyful energy.

정원으로 나가면 유리 공예품으로 인해 수목들이 더 싱그럽게 보였다. 강한 햇빛에 비친 유리는 더욱 반짝이는 면모를 뽐내었다. 시간을 잘 맞추면 유리를 녹여서 작품을 만드는 시연을 처음부터 볼 수 있을 것이다.

The glass artifacts made the trees look more lush and vivid when I went out to the garden. The glass reflected in the strong sunlight showed off a more shiny appearance. If you make the right time, you will be able to see a demonstration of melting glass from the beginning.

아마존 스피어스

치훌리 유리 정원을 보고, 아마존 스피어스로 갔다. 아마존 스피어스는 아마존 직원들의 휴식과 협업을 위한 공간이라서 아무나 들어갈 수 없었다. 내부에 입장하기 위해 시애틀과 포틀랜드 호스트의 인맥을 알아보았으나 아마존에 근무하는 사람이 아무도 없었다. 심지어 그곳 호스트들도 아직 방문하지 못했단다. 나중에 알게 된 사실이지만 일반인을 위해 공개하는 날도 있다고 하였다.

Amazon Spheres

After seeing the Chihuly Glass Garden, I went to Amazon Spheres. Amazon Spheres was a breakout and collaboration space for Amazon employees, so it's not open to just anyone. I tried reaching out to hosts in Seattle and Portland to try to gain access, but no one there worked for Amazon. Even the hosts there haven't visited yet. I found out later that there are days when it is open to the public.

구글 지도로 찾으니 스페이스 니들에서 별로 멀지 않아서 걸어서 도착하였다. 아마존 스피어스는 마치 우주정거장 분위기의 투명한 구슬 같았다. 유리로 만들어진 돔은 도시의 회색 빌딩 사이에서 특별한 존재감을 드러냈다. TV에서 본 것처럼 유리창 너머로 보이는 이국적인 식물들이 작은 정글처럼 얽혀 있었고, 밖에서 보기만 해도 신선한 공기를 내뿜는 듯했다.

들어갈 수는 없었으나 더 잘 보이는 곳은 없을까 살피다가 바로 앞에 있는 아마존 건물로 들어갔다. 우리나라 기업들처럼 제복을 입은 경비원이 입구부터 가로막을 줄 알았는데 아무도 우리를 제지하지 않았다. 1층부터 3층까지 높이 연결된 로비는 넓어서 답답하지 않았다. 퇴근 무렵이라 직원들의 즐거운 웃음소리가 공간을 가득 채웠다.

건너편 아마존 스피어스를 부러운 눈으로 한참 바라보았다. 기업의 심장부 한쪽에 잠시 서 있으니 낯설면서도 묘하게 설레었다. 스피어스는 단순한 건축물이 아니라, 일과 휴식, 사람과 자연을 연결하는 거대한 유리 정원처럼 다가왔다.

I found it on Google Maps and it wasn't far from the Space Needle, so I walked there. The Amazon Spheres looked like transparent marbles reminiscent of a space station. Among the city's gray buildings, the glass dome revealed a special presence. Exotic plants visible through the window, as seen on TV, were intertwined like a small jungle, and even from the outside, they seemed to be breathing fresh air.

I couldn't get in, but I went to the Amazon building right in front of me to see if there was a better place. I thought a uniformed security guard like Korean companies would stop us from the entrance, but no one restrained us. The lobby, which was connected high from the first floor to the third floor, was wide, so it was not stuffy. Around the time of work, the pleasant laughter of the employees filled the space.

I stared enviously at the Amazon Spears across the street. Standing on one side of the corporate heart for a while, I felt strange and strangely excited. The Spheres was not just a structure, but rather a huge glass garden that connects work and relaxation, people and nature.

퍼블릭 마켓

해외여행에서 빠뜨리지 않고 들렀던 곳이 사람 냄새가 나는 재래시장이었다. 나라마다 파는 물건이 조금씩 달라도, 많이 팔려고 애쓰는 상인의 모습이나 흥정하는 고객의 모습은 어느 나라나 매한가지다.

집으로 돌아오는 길에 장을 볼 겸 퍼블릭 마켓에 갔으나 파장 시각이라 먹거리는 별로 없었다. 입구에 들어서면 가운데에 수산물 가게가 크게 차지하고, 오른쪽으로 몇 개의 꽃집을 이어 옷가게, 그림, 기념품 등 수공예품 거리가 이어졌다. 왼쪽에는 건어물과 채소, 반찬 가게 등 먹거리를 팔았다.

시장 주변과 건물 주변에 다양한 레스토랑을 만날 수 있었다. 건물 아래쪽으로 나가면 껌 벽이 나오고, 고가 공원을 지나 워터프론트, 대관람차, 수족관 등으로 이어졌다.

Public market

A place I never missed while traveling abroad was the traditional market with a human touch. Even if the goods sold are slightly different from country to country, the appearance of merchants struggling to sell a lot or customers haggling is the same in every country.

On the way back home, I went to the public market to go grocery shopping, but there was not much food because it was a wavelength time. When I enter the market entrance, a seafood store occupies the center, followed by a few flower shops on the right, followed by a handicraft street such as clothing stores, paintings, and souvenirs. On the left, they sell dried fish, vegetables, and side dishes.

I was able to find a variety of restaurants around the market and the building. A gum wall appeared when I went down the building, passed through an elevated park, and led to a waterfront, a Ferris wheel, and an aquarium.

퍼블릭 마켓 바로 앞에 있는 스타벅스 1호점은 여전히 북적거렸다. 가게가 비좁아서 기념품을 사는 사람이 대부분이고, 음료는 테이크아웃(Take out)만 주문할 수 있었다. 호스트에게 선물할 검은색 텀블러 하나를 샀는데 한국과 비슷한 가격이었다.

퍼블릭 마켓 뒤쪽에 있는, 파머스 마켓 입구에 돼지 동상이 있었다. 뉴욕 월가에는 황소 동상이 트레이드마크라면 시애틀에는 커다란 돼지 동상이 마스코트이다. 우리나라도 돼지가 복을 가져온다고 믿는데, 생각이 비슷한 듯하다. 돼지 동상은 기부함 역할을 하는데, 기부금은 마켓 유지에 쓰인다고 하였다. 돼지 동상은 시애틀 시내 군데군데서 볼 수 있었다.

The first Starbucks store right in front of the public market was still bustling. Most people bought souvenirs because the store was cramped, and drinks could only be ordered to take out. I bought a black tumbler for my host as a gift, and it was similar price to Korea.

There was a pig statue at the entrance to the Farmer's Market, behind the Public Market. If the bull statue is the trademark of Wall Street in New York, then a large pig statue is the mascot of Seattle. In our country, we also believe that pigs bring good luck, and the thinking seems similar. The pig statue serves as a donation box, and a vendor told me that donations go towards the maintenance of the market. Pig statues were found in some parts of downtown Seattle.

버스를 타는 길에 마트에 들렀다. 현지인이나 교포들이 많이 찾는 한국 제품을 골고루 갖추고 있었다. 아마도 K 드라마 영향 때문이리라 생각하였다.

선진국이라고 다 좋은 것만이 아니다. 1인당 국민소득 10만 달러를 넘는 북유럽 국민들 주머니 사정은 두둑하지 않다. 생활비와 집세가 비싸기 때문이다. 월급은 많으나 수입 정도에 따라서 20~45% 세금을 낸다. 대신 대학 학비, 병원 진료, 노인 복지 등이 무료로 잘되어 있어서 노후 생활을 별로 걱정하지 않는다.

시애틀도 별반 다르지 않았다. 사과는 1파운드(약 450g)에 5,200원이었고, 오이 하나 3,500원이었다. 뭔가 사려다가 자꾸 손이 오그라들었다. 물가가 상상을 초월한다. 연봉 억대를 받아도 힘든 삶이라고 하는 말이 피부에 와닿았다. 호스트에게 대접할 불고기용 쇠고기와 채소 몇 개를 샀더니 100불이 넘었다.

사악한 물가에 첫인상과 달리 시애틀이 무서워졌다.

I stopped by a supermarket on the way to the bus. It had a wide selection of Korean products popular with locals and Korean expats. I thought it was probably due to the influence of K-dramas.

Developed countries are not all good. The Nordic country has a GDP of more than $100,000, but its citizens has poor pockets. Because the cost of living and housing rent are expensive. Even if the monthly salary is high, they pay 20-45% tax depending on the level of income. Instead, college tuition, hospital care, and elderly welfare are free, so people do not have to worry much about their retirement life.

Seattle was not much different upper countries. Apples were 5,200 won per pound and cucumbers 3,500 won. My hands kept curling up when I tried to buy something. Prices are beyond my imagination. The words "a life that is hard even if you get paid hundreds of millions of dollars a year" touched my heart. I bought beef for bulgogi and some vegetables for my host and it cost more than 100 dollars.

Contrary to my first impression, Seattle's high prices have made me afraid.

푸드 트럭에서 저녁을

에밀리 가족에게 저녁을 대접하려고 했는데 채식주의자, 탄수화물을 섭취하지 않는 식구도 있어서 대부분 각자 알아서 취향대로 끼니를 해결한다고 하였다. 음식을 대접할 기회가 없어서 섭섭하여 양념에 재어둔 쇠고기만 조금 드렸다.

에밀리 부부를 따라간 곳은 생각지도 못한 푸드트럭이었다. 도로 앞쪽에 편의점이 있고, 뒤쪽 작은 공간에 테이블이 놓여 야외 레스토랑이 된다. 누구의 아이디어였을까. 몇 년 전부터 실시했는데 가격이 일반 레스토랑보다 저렴하고, 날마다 다른 메뉴를 맛볼 수 있어서 주민들도 애용하고, 특히 젊은이들에게 인기가 많다고 하였다. 외식으로라도 대접하고 싶었으나 호스트가 더치페이를 하는 바람에 우리 것만 계산하였다.

집으로 돌아와 선물을 드리니 너무 많다고 놀라워하면서도 기쁨의 웃음은 끊이지 않았다.

Dinner at a food truck

I was going to treat the Emily family to dinner, but some of them are vegetarians or don't eat carbohydrates, so most of them eat their own meals. I were disappointed that I did not have a chance to serve food, so I only gave them a little seasoned beef.

It was an unexpected food truck that followed Emily and her husband. There is a convenience store in front of the road, and a table is placed in a small space behind it to become an outdoor restaurant. Whose idea was it? It was conducted a few years ago, and it was cheaper than regular restaurants, and it was popular with residents because they could taste different menus every day, especially with young people. I wanted to treat the Emily couple even for a meal out, but the host paid Dutch, so we only paid for ours.

I gave the host a present after I came home. They were surprised that there were too many, but the laughter of joy was constant.

시애틀 공립 도서관

오늘날 자신을 만든 것은 마을 도서관이었다는 빌 게이츠의 연설처럼 미국이나 호주에서는 마을 도서관이 주민들의 안방이고, 휴식처 역할을 한다.

해외여행 중에 동네 도서관이나 유명한 도서관을 찾아서 들르곤 하였다. 외관이 선박 모양의 헬싱키 중앙도서관은 오픈 도서관으로 카페, 아이들 놀이터, 공연장, 청소년 만남의 장, 다양한 배움의 공간이 갖추어진 멀티 공간이다. 남녀노소 누구나 애용하는 장소이다.

이집트 알렉산드리아 도서관은 유네스코에서 재건하였다. 도서관 외벽에는 여러 언어가 조각되어 있는데 몇 단어의 한글이 있어서 뿌듯하였다. 이 도서관의 특색은 파피루스로 된 책과 희귀 도서를 많이 소장하고 있다는 점이다.

웅장함이 돋보이는 멜버른 빅토리아 주립도서관은 오페라 무대 공연장을 연상하게 하였다. 스톡홀름 공공도서관은 층고가 높은 3층의 타원형 벽에 빽빽하게 채워진 서가에 압도당하였다. 한국의 도서관도 점점 멀티 공간으로 변모하고 있어서 다행이다.

이곳 도서관은 왜 유명한지 알고 싶어서 시애틀 공립 도서관을 찾아갔다. 프리츠커 건축상을 받은 렘 콜하스(Rem Koolhaas) 교수가 설계하여 우수한 건축물로 여러 번 수상하였다.

Seattle Public Library

Bill Gates said it was the town library that made him what he is today. In the United States and Australia, the town library serves as a home for residents and a resting place.

While traveling abroad, I used to visit local libraries or famous libraries. Helsinki Central Library, which has a ship-shaped exterior, is an open library and is a multi-space with a cafe, children's playground, performance hall, youth meeting hall, and various learning spaces. It is a place frequented by people of all ages and genders.

The Library of Alexandria in Egypt was rebuilt by UNESCO. The outer wall of the library was carved with various languages, and I was proud to have several words of Korean. The special feature of this library is that it has a large collection of papyrus books and rare books.

Melbourne's Victoria State Library, which stands out for its grandeur, was reminiscent of an opera stage. Stockholm Public Library was overwhelmed by bookshelves densely packed with oval walls on the third floor with high stories. It is fortunate that Korean libraries are also transforming into multi-spaces.

I visited the Seattle Public Library because I wanted to know why this library is so famous. Designed by Professor Rem Koolhaas, who received the Pritzker Architecture Award, it has been awarded several times for its excellent architecture.

저게 도서관이라고? 도저히 도서관 건물이라곤 믿기지 않았다. 얼핏 보면 삐딱하게 기울고, 어긋난 블록이 3개의 층으로 나누어져 제멋대로 쌓여있는 듯하였다. 공간 자체가 나에게 끊임없이 질문을 던지는 형식 파괴의 최첨단 건축물이었다.

태양광을 최대한 살리기 위해 철제 구조물에 유리만으로 건축되었다. 부산 영화의전당 한 면의 외곽도 같은 재료를 사용하여 햇빛이 온종일 비치니 항상 밝게 느껴지는 점이 닮았다.

밖에서는 3층인 듯하나 안으로 들어가면 11층 건물이라니 더 놀라웠다. 외관은 무척 아름다운데 입구 주변은 지린내로 코를 막아야 했다. 청소 담당자는 없는 것일까. 도서관 내부에만 집중해서 신경 쓸 것이 아니라 주변에도 관리가 이루어지면 더 좋을 텐데.

도서관 탐색을 하다 보니 내가 정확하게 몇 층에 있는지 알 수가 없었다. 이유는 북스파이럴(Book Spiral) 시스템으로 서가 공간을 나선형으로 만들었기 때문이다. 이곳은 철학, 다음 층은 역사, 다른 층에는 문학 등 서가를 짜서 물리적인 공간으로 책을 꽂아 둔 게 아니었다. 경사로를 따라 십진분류법으로 책을 정렬하였고, 신간을 새로 사들여도 분류법에 맞는 곳에다 꽂을 수 있도록 기존 서가를 그대로 확장할 수 있는 유연성이 돋보이는 미래형 도서관이었다.

Is that a library? I could not believe it was a library building. At first glance, it seemed to lean awkwardly, its three offset blocks appearing to be stacked at random. The space itself was a state-of-the-art structure of destruction that constantly asked me questions.

In order to maximize the sunlight, only glass was built on the steel structure. The outer periphery of one side of the Busan Cinema Center is similar in that it always feels bright because the sunlight shines all day long using the same material.

It looked like it's on the third floor from the outside, but when I went inside, I was more surprised that it was an 11-story building. The exterior was very beautiful, but around the entrance, I had to cover my nose with the smell of urine. Is there anyone in charge of cleaning? It would be better if there were management around the library as well as focusing on the interior of the library.

While searching the library, I could not tell exactly which floor I was on. The reason was that the book spiral system made the space spiral. The book was not put in a physical space by composing books such as philosophy, history on the next floor and literature on the other floor. The books were arranged in decimal classification along the ramp, and it was a futuristic library with the flexibility to expand the existing bookshelves so that they could be inserted where they fit the classification method even if new books were purchased.

도서관 입장은 누구나 가능하였다. 1층에는 카페가 있어서 열심히 공부하다가 커피가 당길 때, 그냥 앉아서 쉬고 싶을 때 이용할 수 있겠다. 4층인지 5층인지 모르겠으나 팩스, 복사, 스캔 등을 갖추고 있는 인터넷이 있었던 공간에는 빈자리가 없었다.

홈리스와 실업자는 영화를 보거나 음악 들으며 하루를 보내고 있었다. 독거노인으로 여겨지는 노인들 역시 기계가 제공하는 즐거움으로 외로움을 삭이고 있었다. 구직자는 구인 공고를 열심히 찾으며 자기 소개장을 쓰고 스캔하여 이메일로 보내기까지 완료하였다. 가난한 이들이 많은 돈 들이지 않고 하루를 보낼 수 있는 공간이 있어서 참 다행이지 않은가.

한국어 외 여러 나라 언어로 된 책을 소장하고 있었다. 이런 책이 도서관에 있어도 되나 싶을 성인용 에로틱한 만화책도 있을 만큼 어마한 양과 다양한 책을 만날 수 있었다.

우리가 방문했던 날에 교복 입은 초등학생들이 체험하러 왔었다. 도서관 예절을 이미 익혔는지 선생님을 따라 살금살금 걷는 모습이 귀여웠다.

Anyone could enter the library. There is a cafe on the first floor, so you can use it when you want to study hard, then when you want to drink coffee, or when you want to sit down and rest. I din't know if it was the 4th or 5th floor, but there was no vacancies in the space with internet access, fax, copy, and scan facilities.

Homeless and the unemployed were taking the day off watching movies or listening to music. The elderly, considered to be the elderly living alone, were also reducing their loneliness with the joy provided by the machine. The job seeker eagerly looked for job openings, wrote a self-introduction letter, scanned it, and sent it by e-mail. Isn't it a relief that there is a space where the poor can spend their days without spending a lot of money?

It had books in various languages, including Korean. I was able to meet a huge amount of books and a variety of books to the extent that there are erotic comic books for adults that might be okay to have such books in the library.

On the day we visited, elementary school students wearing school uniforms came to experience it. It was cute to walk with the teacher to see if they had already learned library etiquette.

항공기 박물관

다른 도시로 이동하는 날, 에밀리가 바쁘다면서도 렌터카 업체로 바래다주었다. 혹시 모를 사고에 대비하여 풀옵션 보험에 가입하고, 한국에서 운전하던 차와 비슷한 SUV 차량을 빌렸다. 필요한 작동법을 익힌 후 출발하였다. 시원하게 뻗은 도로는 차선 간격이 넓어서 운전하기 수월했다.

워싱턴주에는 시애틀 서쪽으로 크고 작은 섬이 많다. 예전에 왔을 때 바라만 보았던 곳, 그중 올림픽 반도에 있는 올림픽산에 가고 싶어서 세큄(Sequim)에 사는 호스트 앤(Ann) 댁을 선택하였다.

오후에 오라는 연락을 받고 시간을 맞추기 위해 타코마공항 부근에 있는 항공기 박물관에 들렀다. 기대 없이 찾아간 박물관은 놀라움의 연속이었다. 정부에서 관리하는 곳이라서 그런지 다른 곳에 비해 저렴한 입장료 14.50달러가 전혀 아깝지 않았다.

주 건물에는 사무실을 비롯하여 기념관과 식당 등 편의시설이 있었고, 큰 전시장에는 수십 종의 비행기를 전시하고 있었다. 작은 전시장에는 전시 주제에 맞는 비행기 모형과 사진 설명으로 빠르게 이해할 수 있었다.

The Museum of Flight

On the day I moved to another city, Emily said she was busy but dropped us to a rental car company. In case of an accident, I paid full-option insurance and rented an SUV similar to the car I was driving in Korea. I started after learning the necessary operation. The wide lanes on the wide, stretch road made driving easy.

Washington state has many large and small islands west of Seattle. I chose Ann's house in Sequim because I wanted to go to the Olympic Mountain on the Olympic Peninsula, a place I had only seen before.

I got a text message to come in the afternoon and stopped by the museum of flight near Tacoma Airport to make time. The museum I walked into without any expectations was full of surprises. It's probably a government-managed location. The $14.50 admission fee, which is cheaper than other places, was not a waste at all.

The main building had convenience facilities such as offices, memorial halls, and restaurants, and dozens of types of airplanes were displayed in the large exhibition hall. In the small exhibition hall, I could quickly understand it with airplane models and photo descriptions that fit the exhibition's theme.

실내 통로를 건너 외부로 나간 후 육교를 지나면 축구장 크기의 격납고 같은 시설이 나왔다. 실제 크기의 여객기, 전 대통령이 사용했던 전용기, 미군이 참전했던 전투기 등에 직접 올라가서 관람하였다.

하늘을 날고 싶다는 인간의 욕망이 우주까지 이어졌다. 라이트 형제가 만든 비행기 복제품부터 세계전쟁 때 사용한 전투기, 현재 여객기 등 미국이 보잉 여객기의 강국이 될 수밖에 없음을 보여주었다.

가장 먼저 달에 착륙한 아폴로 계획부터 최근 발사한 화성 탐사를 위한 우주관에서는 허투루 볼 전시품이 하나도 없었다. 조종사나 우주비행사가 꿈인 학생들은 이곳을 방문한다면 더할 나위 없이 좋은 계기가 될 터이다. 비행기 관련 게임이나 놀이 시설이 별도로 설치되어 있어 견학 온 아이들의 조잘대는 소리가 천장까지 닿았다.

After crossing the indoor passage and going outside, a hangar-like facility the size of a soccer field emerged after passing through the overpass. I climbed onto a full-size passenger airplane, a private jet used by a former president, and a fighter aircraft that the U.S. military had used to participated in the war and observed them.

The human desire to fly extended to space. From replicas of planes made by the Wright brothers to fighter jets used during the World War and current airliners, the United States has shown that Boeing has no choice but to become a powerhouse,

The Apollo program, which was the first to land on the moon, and the recently launched space museum for Mars exploration were all precious exhibits. It would be a great opportunity for students who want to become pilots or astronauts to visit. There were separate airplane-related games and amusement facilities, so the chatter of the children on the field trip reached the ceiling.

PART 3

올림픽 반도

The Olympic Peninsula

포트앤젤레스
Port Angeles

앤 집으로

앤이 소개한 라벤더 농장 근처에 가니 꽃망울에 맺힌 향기가 코끝을 자극하였다. 줄을 맞추어 자라는 라벤더와 허름한 건물이 전부였다. 화려하고 요란스러운 입구로 고객을 유치하려는 우리의 상술과는 전혀 달랐다. 나무라고 부르기엔 너무 작은 키, 거친 들판에서도 뿌리를 내렸다. 한동안 군집으로 꽃을 피우며 곤충과 사람을 불러 모을 것이다. 전성기를 뽐내다 시들고, 다시 1년을 버텨나갈 테지.

해마다 같은 꽃이지만 다르게 피어나듯이 우리의 인생도 마찬가지 아닐까. 나의 삶이 해마다 똑같은 적이 한 번도 없었다. 처음엔 불을 붙이기조차 어려운 모닥불이 점점 타올라 건잡을 수 없을 만큼 뜨거워졌다가 서서히 사그라드는 것처럼. 잘나갔던 시절뿐만 아니라 힘든 시절도 나의 인생이었음을 인정할 나이에 이르렀다. 불안했던 걸음마 시절도, 화려한 전성기도, 느긋한 석양길도 숨길 수 없는 나의 생이라는 것을 받아들여야 한다.

Go to Ann's house

When I went near the lavender farm that Ann introduced, the scent on the flower buds stimulated the tip of my nose. It was all about the rustic buildings and lavender that grew in line. It was completely different from our strategy of attracting customers with a colorful and loud entrance. The lavender plants took root in a rough field, too short to be called a tree. For a while, it will bloom in clusters, attracting insects and people. Plants will endure for another year after they have withered in their prime.

They are the same flowers every year, but just as they bloom differently, isn't our life the same? My life has never been the same every year. At first, the bonfire, which was hard to light, started to burn, getting out of control and then slowly disappearing. I have come to an age where I can accept that both my glory days and my hard times were equally parts of my life. I must accept that it was my life that could not hide my anxious childhood, my splendid heyday, and my laid-back sunset path.

7월이 되어야 꽃이 핀다는 안내를 뒤로하고 차를 돌렸다. 호스트 집으로 가는 길에서 마주한 야생화 들판. 하얀 망사를 덮은 듯한 데이지 꽃밭은 만약 천국이 있다면 들어가는 입구는 이런 풍경이 아닐까. 하얀 데이지 꽃말처럼 모든 고민을 잊게 해줄 것 같은 순수함에 빠졌다. 빨간 집을 배경으로 한참 동안 앵글을 맞추며 놀았다.

이어지는 꽃 들판에 감탄하며 달리다 서다 반복하며 마음껏 사진을 찍었다. 근처에 사는 분이었을까, 가던 길을 멈추고 차에서 내려 우리를 위해 사진사 역할을 해주었다.

뭔가 보답을 하고 싶었으나 감사 인사로 대신하였다. 여행길에서 마주한 작은 친절은 피곤함을 날리는 특효약이다. 생각지도 못한 따뜻한 친절 때문에 여운이 강하게 남았다.

Leaving behind the guidance that flowers will bloom only in July, I turned my car around. On the way to my host's house, I saw a field of wildflowers. Daisy flower garden as if covered with white mesh if there is heaven, wouldn't the entrance look like this? Like the meaning of white daisy flower, I fell in love with purity as if it would make me forget all my worries. I played for a long time taking pictures with the red house in the background.

I took pictures as much as I could, driving or pulling over repeatedly, admiring the ensuing field of flowers. Was it someone who lived nearby? She stopped, got out of the car, and served as a photographer for us.

I wanted to repay something, but I replaced it with a thank you. The small kindness I encountered on my trip is a special medicine to blow away my tiredness. The unexpected warm kindness left a strong lingering impression.

올림픽산 동쪽에 있는 앤 집에 도착하니 5시쯤이었다. 눈이 많이 내리는 곳에 적합한 삼각 지붕을 가진 3층 목조 건물이었다. 도시의 번잡함이 싫어서 이곳에 정착하며 직접 설계하고 지었으니 얼마나 애착이 갈까. 수자원 관련 일을 하던 앤과 올림픽 강에 사는 연어 연구원 데이브(Dave) 직업에 딱 맞는 행복한 보금자리였지 싶다.

생활 인프라가 잘 갖추어져 시골에 살아도 불편한 점이 줄어들면 자연스럽게 인구가 분산될 텐데. 서울 집값이 천정부지로 오른 한국이 벤치마킹해도 좋겠다.

맨 아래층에 화장실이 딸린 부부방과 펜트리가 있고, 2층에는 거실과 부엌, 화장실이 있었다. 우리는 삼각 지붕 아래 3층에서 머물렀다. 곳곳에 창이 많아서 밝고, 2층과 3층이 이어진 층고가 높아서 더 넓게 느껴졌다. 목조인데도 곳곳에 히팅 시스템이 잘되어 있었다. 비 오는 날, 벽난로는 따뜻함은 물론 숨어있던 감성을 불러일으켰다.

하늘을 찌를 듯한 삼나무가 둘러싸인 숲에 살면 하루에도 사계절을 만끽할 수 있지 않을까. 먼 산꼭대기의 만년설이 보이고, 초록 잔디로 덮인 뜰과 곳곳에 피어나는 계절 꽃, 각기 다른 나뭇잎의 색 변화를 볼 수 있는 부부가 몹시 부러웠다. 앤과 데이브 이들 부부는 걱정 없이 석양길을 함께 걷는 편한 친구 같았다.

When I arrived at Ann's house on the north-east side of Olympic Mountains, it was around 5 p.m. It was a three-story wooden building with a triangular roof suitable for snowy areas. How attached, they were to this place as they didn't like the bustle of the city and designed and built themselves! It was a perfect place for Ann's job as a water resource researcher and Dave's job as a salmon researcher on the Olympic Peninsula Rivers.

The population will naturally disperse if the inconvenience of living in the countryside decreases due to the well-equipped living infrastructure. It would be good for Korea, where housing prices in Seoul have skyrockted, could benefit from benchmarketing this.

There was a master bedroom with a bathroom and a pentry on the bottom floor, and a living room, kitchen, and bathroom on the second floor. We stayed on the third floor under a triangular roof. It was bright because there were many windows everywhere, and the second and third floors were connected, so it felt wider. Even though it was wood, the heating system was well established everywhere. On a rainy day, the fireplace evoked not only warmth but also sensitivity.

If you live in a forest surrounded by cedar trees, you will be able to enjoy all four seasons in a day. I was very envious of the couple, who could see the ice cap on the top of the mountain in the distance, and see the garden covered with green grass and seasonal flowers blooming everywhere, and the color changes of different leaves. Ann and Dave seemed like comfortable friends who could walk along the sunset path without worrying.

웰컴 티를 즐기면서 우리가 준비한 선물을 펼치니 부부는 선물의 다양한 종류에 놀라고, 인터넷에서 보았던 것과 비슷하다면서 신기해하였다. 우리가 앤 집을 방문하는 첫 번째 한국인이었다. 그들이 한국 음악을 듣고, 지도를 펼치고, 유튜브와 드라마까지 보며, 한국 관련 공부를 얼마나 많이 했는지, 대화 속에서 알 수 있었다. 집 안팎을 청소하고 손님을 맞이하는 우리네 정성과 닮았다.

미국은 중학교에서부터 실용적인 과목을 선택할 수 있어서 남자도 요리하고, 여자도 잔디를 깎거나 자동차를 스스로 고치는 경우를 종종 보았다. 요리를 좋아하고 잘하는 데이브가 그날 저녁 식사를 담당하였다. 바깥에 놓인 바비큐 기구로 구운 연어는 야들하면서 쫀득하여 아이슬란드나 노르웨이 고급 레스토랑에서 먹었던 맛에 뒤지지 않았다.

비가 내리지 않았으면 야외에서 만찬을 즐겼을 텐데 아쉬웠다. 한국 가요와 빗소리를 들으며 대화를 이어갔다. 디저트로 아이스크림까지 풀코스로 먹으니 귀한 손님으로 대접받은 느낌이었다.

드라마 「폭삭 속았수다」를 영어 버전으로 시청하였다. 우리가 사는 제주가 배경이 된 이야기라서 부부가 더욱 흥미를 보였다. 무슨 뜻인지 그들이 잘 모르는 장면을 설명해 줄 수 있어서 우리도 뿌듯하였다.

As they enjoyed the welcome tea and unfolded the gifts we prepared, the couple was surprised by the variety of gifts and was amazed that they were similar to what they had seen on the Internet. We were the first Koreans to visit Ann's house. We could tell from their conversations how much they had studied Korea: listening to Korean music, unfolding maps, watching YouTube videos and dramas. It resembles our sincerity in cleaning up and welcoming guests inside and outside the house.

In the United States, practical subjects can be chosen from middle school, so men cook, and women often mow grass or fix cars themselves. Dave, who loves to cook and is good at cooking, was in charge of the dinner that day. The salmon baked with a barbecue stove outside was tender and chewy, so it was second to none to the taste of eating at high-end Icelandic or Norwegian restaurants.

It was a shame that we could not enjoy dinner outdoors if it had not rained. We continued our conversation while listening to K-pop and rain. We felt like we were treated as a precious guest as we ate ice cream as a full course for dessert.

Together, we watched the drama 「When life gives you tangerines」 in an English version. It was a story set in Jeju, where we live, so they showed much interest. We were also proud to be able to explain a scene they didn't know what it meant.

크레센트 호수에서 트레킹

올림픽산이 그리스에만 있는 줄 알았는데, 거대한 빙하를 품고 있는 올림픽산이 미국에도 있었다. 경관이 수려하고, 희귀한 동식물이 많다. 지역이 광활하여 다양한 트레킹 코스가 있었다. 시애틀과 밴쿠버에서도 보이는 장소이고, 워낙 유명하여 평소에도 찾는 사람이 많다고 하였다.

시애틀 서쪽, 올림픽 반도에 있는 올림픽 공원은 약 3,800㎢이다. 우리나라 서울시의 6배 정도로 광활한 크기로 산, 숲, 호수, 해안, 빙하 등 모든 생태계를 다 갖춘 곳이다.

1938년 루스벨트 대통령 시대 때 국립공원으로, 1976년 유네스코 국제생태 보존지역으로 지정되었다. 1982년에는 유네스코 세계문화유산으로 등재될 만큼 동식물의 보고이며 원시림이 잘 보존된 장소이다. 연간 3,400㎜ 이상의 강수량을 가진 이곳에 신비로운 '호 우림(Hoh Rain Forest)' 온대 우림 지역은 명성이 자자하여 영화 「트와일라잇」의 배경이 되었다.

세계 어디든지 후손들에게 물려줄 자연이 더 훼손되지 않도록 보호할 의무가 우리에게 있다. 더 늦지 않게 모든 나라의 지도자들이 지구 파괴의 심각성을 깨닫고 의미 있게 행동해 준다면 얼마나 다행일까.

사소한 것에서 우리는 행복을 느낀다. 비 내리는 날, 음악과 함께 느긋하게 먹은 아침이 얼마 만인지. 바쁘게 후닥닥거리며 쳇바퀴 돌듯이 보낸 하루의 일상들이 주마등처럼 지나갔다.

Trekking at Lake Crescent

I thought Mount Olympus was only in Greece, but there is also Olympic mountain in the United States, each with a massive glacier. The scenery is beautiful and there are many rare animals and plants. The area was vast, so there were various trekking trails. It is a place that can be seen in Seattle and Vancouver, and it is said that there are many people who usually visit it because it is such a famous mountain.

The Olympic National Park on the Olympic Peninsula, west of Seattle, is about 3,800 square kilometers long. It is vast area, about six times the size of Seoul Korea, and has all kinds of ecosystems, including mountains, forests, lakes, coasts, and glaciers.

It was designated as a national park under President Roosevelt in 1938, and as a UNESCO International Ecological Conservation Area in 1976. It is a treasure trove of flora and fauna, and a place with well-preserved primeval forests, so much that it was inscribed on the UNESCO World Heritage List in 1982. The mysterious 'Hoh Rain Forest' temperate rainforest area is famous and became the setting for the movie 「Twilight」.

We have a duty to protect nature that will be passed down to future generations anywhere in the world from further damage. It would be a great relief if the leaders of all countries realized the seriousness of the destruction of the earth and acted meaningfully before it was too late.

From the smallest things, we feel happy. It's been a while since I had a relaxing breakfast with music on a rainy day. The daily lives that we spent busily chatting with each other passed by like a beacon light.

비가 흩뿌리고 있었지만 앤이 추천한 크레센트 호수(Lake Crescent)로 갔다. 집에서 45분 소요된다고 내비게이션이 안내하였으나 초행이라 1시간 넘게 걸려 도착하였다. 풍광이 뛰어나고 수상 스포츠나 트레킹을 할 수 있어 캠핑장과 콘도는 늘 만원이란다. 식당과 화장실 등 편의시설까지 갖추고 있어 우리가 도착했을 때도 사람들이 많았다.

빙하가 녹아서 이루어진 호수라 물이 맑고 깨끗하여 수초들이 잘 보인다고 하였으나 날씨가 흐려 제 모습을 다 보여주진 않았다. 두 산의 꼭짓점과 맞닿은 호수 위로 피어오르는 안개 자욱한 산수화를 보며 가장 짧은 트레킹을 시작하였다.

목적지 메리미어(Marymere) 폭포로 향하였다. 제주 올레나 오름에 가면 야자 매트가 깔려있거나 나무 데크, 돌계단 등 슬리퍼를 신어도 될 만큼 정비가 잘되어 편하게 다닐 수 있다. 뭔가 아쉽고 이건 아니다 싶었는데 그 이유를 이곳에서 알게 되었다.

이곳에는 매트나 계단 같은 인공물은 볼 수 없었고, 사람이 다닐 만큼의 좁은 길이나 있었다. 보행하기 쉽게 길가의 수목을 제거한 흔적도 없었고, 안내판도 딱 필요한 곳에만 있어서 나는 길을 잘못 들기도 하였다.

It was raining, but we went to Lake Crescent, which Ann recommended. The navigation informed us that it would take 45 minutes from home, but it took more than an hour because it was my first time. Campgrounds and condos are always full because of the excellent scenery and water sports or trekking. There were even convenient facilities such as restaurants and toilets, so there were many people when we arrived.

It was said that the water plants could be seen well because the water was clear and clean because it was a lake made up of melting glaciers, but the weather was cloudy and it did not show all of its appearance. I began the shortest trek, admiring the misty landscape painting rising above the lake where the two mountains meet.

I headed to the destination Marymere Falls. If you go to Olle Trail or Oreum in Jeju, there is a palm mat, or a wooden deck, and a stone staircase. So you can travel comfortably because it is well maintained enough to wear slippers. I felt something was unfortunate and thought this was not right, but I learned the reason here.

Artificial built by humans such as mats and stairs were not visible here, and there were narrow roads enough for people to walk. There was no sign of removing trees on the side of the road for easy walking, and the information board was only where it was needed, so I took the wrong path.

한국에서는 국립공원 관리라는 명목으로, 잡풀이나 억새를 베기도 하고, 야자 매트를 까는 등 정비한다고 하지만 모두가 인간 편의를 위한 관리 차원이었으리라. 자연보호를 위한 진정한 관리나 방책이 필요하지 않을까.

연 강수량이 많은 곳인 데다 그날도 비가 내려 아주 습했다. 거대한 나무들이 뒤엉켜 하늘을 가리고, 초록 카펫이 깔린 원시림으로 이루어진 숲. 주렁주렁 연둣빛과 초록색 이끼 붙은 나뭇가지는 거인이 소매를 펄럭이듯 생명력이 넘쳐났다.

햇빛이 잘 들지 않은 숲은 신비로운 영화 속 장면과 다르지 않았다. 인간의 손길이 닿지 않은 웅장함 속에 느껴지는 고요함이 나를 감싸는 듯한 안정감을 주었다. 이끼 낀 나무를 쓰다듬고 있는 스스로를 발견하고 피식 웃음이 나왔다. 우리는 발걸음을 죽이며 그들이 내뿜는 산소를 마시고, 습한 공기 속에서 느껴지는 흙냄새와 풀 내음을 맡았다. 고요한 천연 숲으로 걷는 자체만으로도 힐링이 되었다.

이끼와 달리 군데군데 자연스럽게 생긴 검붉은색 그루터기는 서서히 분해되며 자연으로 돌아가는 중이었다. 가장 먼저 이들을 분해하는 크고 작은 버섯들이 나무에 둥지를 틀며 존재감을 드러내었다.

대륙답게 큰 고사리도 만났고, 제주서 자주 보았던 나무와 풀도 훨씬 키가 컸다. 나이를 알 수 없는 뿌리가 드러난 고목은 뿌리 크기가 내 키의 몇 배로 사진가들의 좋은 소재가 되었다. 사진을 보니 거대한 자연 앞에서 인간이 얼마나 미미한 존재인지 눈에 확연히 드러났다.

In Korea, in the name of managing national parks, people cut grass or silver grass, put palm mats on the road for maintenance etc., but isn't everyone's management for human convenience. Shouldn't real management or measures be needed for nature conservation?

It was a place with a lot of annual precipitation, and it was very humid that day due to rain. A forest of primeval forests with green carpets, with huge trees intertwined to cover the sky. The branches with green light and green moss were full of life like giants flapping their sleeves.

The sunless forest was no different from the scenes in the mysterious movie. The stillness felt in the grandeur untouched by humans gave me a sense of stability that seemed to surround me. When I found myself stroking a mossy tree, I laughed. We took our steps to breathe in the oxygen they emitted, and we smelled the smell of soil and grass in the moist air. Walking in the calm natural forest itself was healing.

Unlike the moss, the naturally occurring dark red stumps here and there were slowly decomposing and returning to nature. First, large and small mushrooms that break these down reveal their presence by nesting in the trees.

I met a large bracken like a continent, and the trees and grass I often saw in Jeju were much taller. Old trees with unknown roots were several times my height, making them a good subject for photographers. The picture clearly revealed how insignificant humans are in front of huge nature.

MARYMERE FALLS
NO PETS, WEAPONS
OR VEHICLES

질퍽거리는 길을 걷는 내내 귀 기울여 숲의 소리를 감지하였다. 빗방울에 반응하는 풀잎의 움직임을 들으면서, 새소리에 응답하는 바람 소리를 따라 오르막을 올랐다. 물에 부딪히는 자갈의 움직임도 숲의 오케스트라 일부였다.

작은 외나무다리를 건너고 다시 오르막을 올라 마침내 삼 층으로 흘러내리는 폭포에 도착하였다. 빙하가 녹아 흘러내려서일까. 폭포 소리는 경쾌하고 시원한 노랫가락이 되었다. 물이 떨어지는 바위 주변에 생긴 연두색 이끼와 덩굴 식물이 푸르름을 더했다. 애써 비우려 하지 않아도 숲과 폭포가 알아서 쓱~~ 비워주는 느낌을 만끽하였다.

While walking along the muddy path, I listened carefully to detect the sound of the forest. I climbed uphill following the sound of the wind in response to the sound of birds, listening to the grass' movement in response to the raindrops. The movement of gravel hitting the stream water was also part of the forest orchestra.

After crossing a small single-tree bridge, I climbed again and finally reached the waterfall. The waterfall appeared to be on the third floor. The sound of the waterfall became a cheerful and cool song, maybe because the glacier melted and flowed down. Light green moss and vine plants formed around the falling rocks added green. I enjoyed the feeling that the forest and waterfall emptying themselves without me having to try hard to empty them.

점심시간이 훨씬 지나 크레스켄트 호수로 돌아오는 길에 사슴을 보았다. 제주 오름을 다니면서 노루를 만난 적이 종종 있었는데 여기서도 보니 반가웠다. 한가로이 풀을 뜯는 사슴은 무슨 걱정이 있을까.

5월인데도 비가 오니 초겨울 날씨같이 쌀쌀했다. 점심을 먹기 위해 들어간 레스토랑 안은 벽난로 훈기로 넘쳤다. 호수가 보이는 창가에 앉아 샐러드와 정성이 들어간 수제 버거로 꿀맛 같은 점심을 먹었다.

밖으로 나와 마주한 맑게 갠 하늘과 호수는 막 도착해서 만났던 모습과 달랐다. 짧게 마주한 윤슬의 반짝임과 짙푸른 물결에 그동안 복잡했던 마음을 흘려보냈다. 맑아진 날씨 덕분에 더 멋진 추억을 안겨준 배경을 한껏 즐겼다.

I saw a deer on my way back to Lake Creskent long after lunchtime. I often met roe deer while going to Jeju Oreum, and it was nice to see them here as well. What worries do deer who are grazing leisurely?

It was raining even in May, so it was chilly like early winter weather. The restaurant I went to for lunch, Lake Crescent Lodge, was full of fireplace warmth. I sat by the window overlooking the lake and had a delicious lunch with salad and handmade burgers.

The clear sky and the lake that I came out and met were different from the way we had just arrived. The brief encounter withl lake's sparkle and the deep blue waves made me let go of my complicated feelings. I fully enjoyed the background that would bring me more wonderful memories thanks to the clear weather.

다른 도시로 이동하는 날이면 긴장한 탓인지 더 일찍 잠에서 깨었다. 부엌으로 내려가 점심때 먹을 샌드위치를 조용히 만들었다. 앤이 차려준 마지막 아침이 더 맛있는 날이었다.

만나면 헤어지는 일이 다반사인데 아직도 헤어지는 일에 어색하다. 특히 서바스 호스트와의 헤어짐에 서투르다. 이틀 동안 앤 부부와 많은 이야기를 나누며 언니처럼 친구처럼 정이 들었다. 앤도 그런 마음이었을까.

그녀가 라벤더 향 비누를 선물로 주었다. 비누가 닳아 없어질 때까지 앤의 고마움을 생각할 것이다. 둘이 나누어 먹으라는 훈제 연어는 밴쿠버 마지막 호스트네에 다시 선물로 드렸다. 울컥했던 마음을 숲에다 묻어두고 남쪽으로 향하였다. 평화로우면서 웅장했던 올림픽산이 그리워질 것이다.

I woke up earlier on the day I moved to another city, maybe because I was nervous. I went down to the kitchen and made a sandwich for lunch. The last morning that Ann prepared for me was a more delicious day.

It is common to part ways when we meet people during our travels, but I still feel awkward about it. In particular, I am not good at parting ways with the host of Servas. For two days, I talked a lot with Ann and Dave, so got close like a friend and sister. Did Ann feel the same me?

She gave us a lavender soap as a gift. I will feel gratitude for Ann until the soap wears off. Also they gave us smoked salmon to share. We gave it to the last host who stayed in Vancouver. I buried my emotional feelings in the forest and headed south. I will miss the peaceful and magnificent Olympic Mountain.

레이니어산으로

레이니어산(Mountain Ranier)을 거쳐 포틀랜드까지 가는 일정이다. 제주도 면적 두 배 가까운 올림픽 반도를 빠져나오는 데 거의 두 시간이 걸렸다. 산이 높아서 그런지 비가 내렸다가 맑아졌다가, 안개가 꼈다가 폭우가 쏟아지는 등 종잡을 수 없는 날씨로 운전대에 힘이 들어갔다.

레이니어산 가는 길 도중, 작은 마을 애쉬포드에는 기차 두 량을 개조하여 만들어진 숙소와 레스토랑이 있었다. 시간이 많았다면 기차 레스토랑에서 커피라도 마셨을 텐데….

갔던 날이 일요일이라 부근에 장이 열렸다. 다양한 수공예품을 파는 가게에는 손님이 한 명도 없었고, 체리 파는 곳에는 손님이 줄을 이었다. 먹고사는 일이 어쩔 수 없는 인간의 기본 욕구임을 인정해야 했다. 우리도 체리 한 바구니 10달러에 사서 며칠 동안 비타민을 공급받았다.

To Rainier Mountain

It is a journey to Portland via Mountain Ranier. It took almost two hours to get out of the Olympic Peninsula, which is twice the size of Jeju Island. Perhaps because the mountain is high, it rained and cleared, foggy and heavy rain poured down, which forced the steering wheel.

On the way to Mount Rainier, in the small town of Ashford, there were accommodations and restaurants built from the renovation of two trains. If I had a lot of time, I would have had coffee at the train restaurant···.

The day I went was Sunday, so there was a market open nearby. There were no customers in the shop selling various handicrafts, but there was a line of customers at the place selling cherries. We had to admit that making a living is a basic human need. We also bought a basket of cherries for $10 and received vitamins for a few days.

입장료를 내고 레이니어산 국립공원에 들어서자 공기가 다르게 느껴졌다. 청량한 공기로 인해 힐링이 되는 듯 긴 운전으로 인한 긴장감이 사라졌다.

목적지 레인보우 로지까지 또 1시간이 걸렸다. 수북이 쌓인 눈을 마주하니 봄에서 겨울로 계절이 거꾸로 가는 듯하였다. 눈을 볼 거라는 생각을 못 했는데 놀랍기도 하고 걱정이 살짝 되었다. 아래쪽에는 비가 내리는데 고도가 높아지자 잠깐 눈이 흩날렸다. 제주 5·16도로만큼 구불구불한 길을 한참 운전하여 설국으로 된 방문 센터에 다다랐다.

워싱턴주의 심장이라 불릴 만큼 해발 약 4,400m의 높은 곳에서 존재감을 드러내었다. 만년설로 덮인 봉우리와 그를 둘러싼 2,000m가 넘는 여러 산이 시샘하듯 높이를 뽐내고 있었다. 일 년 내내 만년설로 덮여 있어서 어떤 계절에 와도 멋진 경치를 볼 수 있겠다.

밖으로 나오니 손이 시릴 정도로 찬 공기에 몸이 움츠러들었다. 헨리 잭슨 기념관 방문 센터(Henly M. Jackson Memorial Visitor Center)에서 시작되는 트레킹 코스가 여러 개 있으니 등산객 능력에 맞는 곳으로 선택하면 될 터이다.

The air felt different when I entered Rainier Mountain National Park after paying an admission fee. The tension caused by the long driving disappeared as if it were healing due to the fresh air.

It took another hour to get to the destination Rainbow Lodge. Facing the piles of snow, I felt like the seasons were going backwards from spring to winter. I didn't think I would see snow, I was surprised and a little worried. It's raining down below, but it snowed for a while as the altitude increased. I drove a long time on a winding road like the Jeju 5.16 road and arrived at the snowy visiting center.

It was magnificently present at a height of about 4,400m above sea level, enough to be called the heart of Washington state. The peak covered with ice caps and several mountains over 2,000m surrounding it boasted of their height. It is covered with ice caps all year round, so no matter what season we come, we can see a wonderful view.

When I came out the car, the cold air made my body shrink. There are several trekking courses that start at the Henry M. Jackson Memorial Visitor Center, so you can choose a place that suits your hikers' abilities.

차림새나 피부가 다양한 사람들이 눈 쌓인 고지를 향해 오르는 모습이 우리를 자극하였다. 정상에 가면 백록담처럼 눈 덮인 분화구를 볼 수 있을까. 설피를 신고 완전 무장으로 꼭대기까지 가는 사람들이 부러웠다. 용기를 내어 우리도 한 발 한 발 걸었다. 눈이 쌓였어도 다행히 길이 미끄럽지 않아 200m 정도까지 올랐다.

성벽을 지키듯 서 있는 소나무들이 마치 바람 앞에서도 흔들림 없는 병정처럼 꼿꼿하였다. 눈꽃이 핀 소나무 사이로 보이는 풍경은 온통 눈이 덮여 마치 다른 세상처럼 고요하고 평화로웠다. 차가운 공기 속에서 빛나는 설경은 고요함 속에서도 묵직한 힘이 느껴졌다.

나뭇가지 위의 눈꽃과 뾰족한 잎을 드러낸 초록색이 잘 어울려 인간이 만들 수 있는 한계를 초월한 아름다움을 보여주었다. 산 아래로 펼쳐진 전경과 꼭대기에 눈 모자를 쓴 먼 산 경치는 이승이 아닌 딴 세상이었다. 레이니어산은 감히 근접할 수 없는 그 자체만으로도 삶과 죽음을 품은 위대한 생명의 표상이었다.

봄에 느끼는 겨울을 만끽하고, 방문 센터에서 준비해 온 점심을 먹었다. 센터 2층에서 레이니어산 안내도와 사진 등에서 이곳에 살던 인디언 삶의 역사를 알 수 있었다. 귀한 동식물과 지질학적 가치, 만년설 등이 국립공원으로 지정된 이유였음을 사진을 통해 알 수 있었다. 다음에 기회가 온다면 단단히 채비하여 레이니어산 꼭대기까지 도전해야겠다.

The sight of people of all shapes and colors climbing up the snow-covered hills was inspiring. Can we see a snow-covered crater like Baeknokdam in Halla Mt. when we go to the top? I envied people who went all the way to the top wearing snowflakes. We mustered up our courage and walked step by step. Even though the snow piled up, fortunately, the road was not slippery, so we climbed to about 200m.

The pine trees standing guard as if guarding the castle walls stood upright like soldiers who could not be shaken even in the wind. The scenery seen through the snow-flowered pine trees was all covered with snow, so it was calm and peaceful as if it were a different world. The snow scene shining in the cold air felt a heavy power even in the stillness.

The snowflakes on the branches and the green color that revealed the pointed leaves went well together, showing the beauty beyond the limits that humans can make. The view of the mountain below and the view of the distant mountain at the top were not this world, but a different world. Mount Rainier was a symbol of a great life with life and death in itself, which could not be dared to approach.

I enjoyed the winter that I felt in spring and ate lunch that I had prepared at the visiting center. On the second floor of the center, I could see the history of Indian life here from the guide map of Mount Rainier and photos. Through the photos, I was able to see that the precious flora and fauna, geological value, and perennial snow were the reasons for designating it as a national park. If I get a chance next time, I should get ready well and challenge myself to the top of Mount Rainier.

포틀랜드

Portland

호스트 린 댁으로

자세히 검색하고 왔으면 레이니어산에서 하루를 머물며 힐링 시간을 더 가졌을 텐데…. 아쉬움을 가득 안고 포틀랜드로 향하였다.

넓은 영토를 가진 나라답게 고속도로나 지방도로가 넓어 운전하기가 수월하였다. 시내로 들어오니 퇴근 시간이라 차가 막혔다. 5시경 도착 예정이었는데 출발부터 늦은 데다 오는 도중에 비도 내리고, 차량 증가로 인해 거의 6시가 되어 도착하였다.

우리를 기다렸던 호스트 린(Lynn)과 남편 테리(Terry)와 인사만 하고 함께 큰 마트로 갔는데 6시에 문을 닫아서 근처 다른 슈퍼에서 장을 보았다. 오리건주는 소비세가 없어서 시애틀에 비하면 물가가 저렴하였다. 뉴욕이나 시애틀에서 은퇴 후 물가가 싼 포틀랜드로 이주하는 사람들이 제법 있다고 하였다. 우리는 넉넉하게 장을 보았다. 특히 주먹보다 큰 애플망고 8개가 든 한 박스를 8달러에 샀으니 횡재한 셈이었다.

두 분 다 교사였던 부부는 아들만 두 명이다. 린은 교사를 하다가 출산으로 그만두고, 아이를 키우면서 상담사가 되어 현재도 일하고 있었다. 관절이 좋지 않은 테리를 위해 집 안에 리프트 시설과 운동하게끔 헬스 기구가 가득한 방이 따로 있었다.

린이 저녁 시간에도 종종 출장 상담이나 온라인 상담으로 일을 해서 대부분 저녁 준비는 테리 차지다. 테리는 익숙한 솜씨로 미트볼을 듬뿍 넣은 스파게티를 순식간에 만들었다. 테리가 음식을 만들 동안 우리는 쇠고기를 손질해서 불고기용으로 재어 놓았다.

To host Lynn's house

If I had searched in detail, I would have stayed one night in Mount Rainier and had more healing time···. Full of regret, we headed to Portland.

As a country with a large territory, it was easy to drive because the highways and local roads were wide. When I came into the city, the roads became congested because it was rush hour. It was scheduled to arrive around 5 o'clock, but it was late from the departure, and it rained on the way, and it arrived at almost 6 o'clock due to the increase in vehicles.

We just said hello to host Lynn and her husband Terry, who waited for us, and went to a big mart together, but it closed at 6 p.m., we went another supermarket nearby. Oregon had no consumption tax, so prices were cheaper than Seattle. It is said that there are quite a few people who move to Portland, where the cost of living is lower, after retiring from New York or Seattle. We had plenty of grocery shopping. In particular, a box of eight apple mangoes larger than my fist was bought for $8 so it was windfall.

The couple, both of whom were teachers, have two sons. Lynn was a teacher and quit because of childbirth, raising her child, becoming a counselor and still working. For Terry, who had bad joints, there was a separate room in the house full of exercise equipment and a lift.

Most dinners are Terry's because Lynn often works through business or online counseling even during the evening. Terry used to make spaghetti with a lot of meatballs in an instant. While Terry was cooking, we trimmed the beef and measured it for bulgogi.

오랜만에 먹는 스파게티 맛은 일품이었다. 린과 잔을 부딪치며 마신 화이트와인은 스파게티와도 궁합이 잘 맞았다. 저녁 후에 선물을 드리고 린의 안내로 집을 구경하였다.

도로에서 보이는 2층 현관 왼쪽에 식당 겸 거실이 보이고, 그 뒤에 서쪽과 남쪽으로 창이 난 부엌에 일몰의 햇살이 부드럽게 쏟아졌다. 부엌 맞은쪽에 TV를 품은 커다란 거실이 있었다.

현관 옆에는 차고였다. 차고 안 작은 냉장고에는 맥주, 와인, 주스 등 음료 종류가 가득 있었다. 먹거리를 항상 넉넉하게 준비하는 것 같았다. 현관 안에서 오른쪽으로 테리가 애용하는 방이 있었다. 그가 만든 레고 작품과 피규어 작품에서 섬세하고 꼼꼼한 테리의 성격을 엿볼 수 있었다.

계단을 내려간 1층에는 여러 개의 방과, 화장실, 펜트리 등이 있었다. 린의 작업 방에 들어서면 보물 1호로 보이는 재봉틀이 눈에 먼저 띈다. 자식만큼이나 애지중지 여겼을 테지. 한쪽 벽면을 차지한 긴 수납장에는 작품을 만들고 남은 천 조각이 차곡차곡 쌓여 있었다. 그녀는 그 문을 열 때마다 추억 하나씩 꺼내 보는 심정이 아닐까.

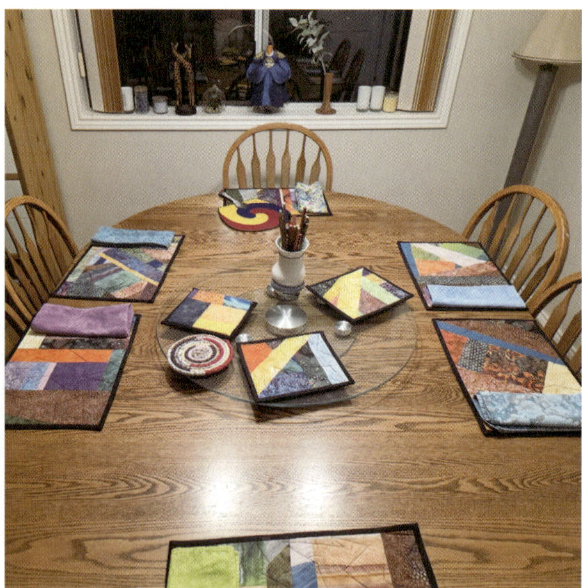

Spaghetti that I haven't eaten in a long time was really delicious. The white wine I drank while bumping a glass with Lynn went well with spaghetti. After dinner, I gave a gift and looked around the house with Lynn's guidance.

There was a dining room and living room on the left side of the entrance on the second floor from the street, and the sun of sunset poured gently into the kitchen with windows to the west and south. There was a large living room with a TV opposite the kitchen.

Next to the front door was a garage. The small refrigerator in the garage was full of drinks such as beer, wine, and juice. It seemed that they prepared always plenty of food. On the right side of the front door was Terry's favorite room. Terry's delicate and meticulous personality was shown in his Lego and figure works.

On the first floor down the stairs, there were several rooms, toilets, and a pantry. When I enter Lynn's studio, the sewing machine, which appears to be Treasure No. 1, stands out first. She must have loved it as much as her child. In a long cabinet that occupied one wall, there were stacked pieces of fabric left after she made the work. Wouldn't she feel like taking out a memory every time she opened the door?

뒤뜰로 내려가는 입구부터 아름다운 꽃들이 반기더니 뒤뜰에도 만발하였다. 뒤뜰 한 쪽에서 여러 가지 채소를 키우고 있었다. 우리를 환영하기 위해 게스트룸에 꽂아둔 진기한 꽃에서 린의 정성을 보았다.

린은 손재주가 뛰어났다. 재봉틀을 이용하여 조각보처럼 자투리 천을 연결하여 침대 커버, 테이블보, 다양한 소품을 만드는 퀼트 솜씨가 보통이 아니었다. 천 조각으로 나무, 동물 등으로 표현할 정도로 색감 사용이나 아이디어가 특출하였다. 집 안 곳곳에서 그녀의 예술적 감각을 살린 작품들이 있었다. 그녀는 손수 만든 주황색 계열의, 세상에서 하나뿐인 냄비 받침을 우리에게 선물로 주었다.

주부, 상담사, 간호사, 사회활동가 등 1인 몇 역할을 하는 린에게서 엄마라는 위대함을 느꼈다. 쾌활한 성격과 자신감 넘치는 언변 뒷면에 숨겨진 외로움을 읽을 수 있었다. 가족을 위해 끊임없이 인내하고 노력하며, 열심히 사는 그녀에게서 나를 보는 듯해서 강한 연민을 느꼈다. 여자의 일생은 동서양 구분 없이 다 저런 것일까.

Beautiful flowers greeted us from the entrance to the backyard, and they were in full bloom in the backyard. She was growing various vegetables on one side of the backyard. To welcome us, we saw Lynn's sincerity in the rare flowers placed in the guest room.

Lynn was very dexterous. She demonstrated remarkable quilting skills by connecting small pieces of cloth like a patchwork cloth using a sewing machine to make bed covers, tablecloths, and various props. The use of colors and ideas were so exceptional that they were expressed as wood or animals with pieces of cloth.There were works that utilized her artistic sense throughout the house. She gave us a hand-made orange-colored, the only thing in the world a hot pad as a gift.

I felt the greatness of being a mother from Lynn, who plays several roles per person, including a housewife, counselor, nurse, and social activist. I could read the loneliness behind her cheerful personality and confident speech. I felt a strong sense of pity for her, seeing myself in her, who constantly persevered, worked hard, and lived diligently for her family. Is a woman's life like that regardless of whether it's in the East or the West?

아카디아 비치

원래 계획은 어제 레이니어산에 갔다가 오는 길에 캐넌 비치에 들러서 일몰을 보고 나서, 린 집에 오려고 했었다. 그렇게 했다면 9시 넘어 도착하게 되는데, 처음 방문하는 남의 집에 너무 늦게 가는 것이 실례가 될 것 같아서 포기하였다.

오후에는 차가 막혀서 아침 일찍 갔다가 빨리 돌아오기로 하였다. 린 댁에서 북서쪽에 있는 바다까지 약 1시간 30분이 소요되었다.

캐넌 비치를 가기 전에 린이 알려준 해안가로 가려했으나 찾지 못하고, 도착한 곳이 아카디아 비치(Arcadia beach)였다. 부산이나 제주의 바다처럼 도로 옆에 있는 것이 아니라 도로에서 한참 내려가야 했다. 주차장에 차를 세우고 숲속을 지나 누군가 놓아둔 사다리로 내려가 바닷가에 닿았다.

밴쿠버 잉글리시 베이처럼 숲 쪽으로 통나무들이 많았다. 저 나무들은 어디서 왔을까. 긁히고 찍혀 살이 드러난 나무는 사람들의 의자가 되어주었다. 남은 생을 살다가 자연으로 돌아가겠지.

사람들에게 덜 알려진, 때 묻지 않은 바닷가는 한적하였다. 물이 덜 빠진 바닷가는 거울이 되어 모든 것을 반영시켰다. 그곳에 하늘이 내려앉아 푸른빛을 뿜어내었다. 맨몸으로 드러난 바닷가를 무대 삼고, 파도 소리를 음향 삼아, 신난 아이처럼 춤을 추었다.

Arcadia Beach

My original plan was to stop by Cannon Beach on the way back from Mount Rainier, watch the sunset yesterday, and then come to Lynn's house. If I did, I would arrive past 9, but I gave up because I thought it would be rude to go to someone's house too late for the first time.

In the afternoon, there was traffic, so I decided to go early in the morning and return quickly. It took about an hour and a half from Lynn's house to the sea in the northwest.

Before going to Cannon Beach, I tried to go to the waterfront that Lynn told me, but I couldn't find it, and I arrived at Arcadia Beach. It was not on the side of the road like Busan or the sea of Jeju, had to go down the road for a long time. I pulled up in the parking lot, passed through the forest, went down to a ladder placed by someone and reached the beach.

Like Vancouver English Bay, there were many logs toward the forest. Where did those trees come from? The trees that were scratched and stamped with flesh became people's chairs. They will return to nature after living the rest of their lives.

Less well-known, unspoiled beaches were deserted. The beach, which was less drained, became a mirror and reflected everything. The sky fell there and emitted a blue light. Using the bare beach as the stage and the sound of the waves as the sound, I danced like an excited child.

차가운 공기를 머금은 해안에 희뿌연 안개가 내려앉으니 바다는 은은한 회색으로 물들었다. 차갑게 부서지는 파도가 가져다주는 것은 고작 모래뿐인데 생생한 감각으로 내 발끝을 깨웠다. 무한한 공간 속에서 잠시나마 나를 둘러싼 모든 소음이 사라지는 듯하였다.

끝없이 이어지는 해안선을 따라 걸었다. 파도 소리만이 가만가만 귀에 닿는 곳, 멀리 보이는 자욱하게 안개 낀 바다는 수채화 풍경이 되었다. 개를 데리고 산책 나온 사람도, 파도에 휩쓸려 침식과 퇴적작용을 보여주는 모래밭도 수채화 속으로 들어갔다.

한참 걷다가 우연히 예쁜 조약돌을 발견하였다. 누구나 좋아할 만한 모양 하트. 누가 언제 이렇게 예쁜 모양을 만들었지? 손으로 꺼내면 하트 모양이 아닐 것을 알기에 눈으로만 감상하였다. 그것도 잠시, 밀려온 파도는 질투하듯 순식간에 모래로 덮어 흔적조차 남기지 않았다.

As a mist of gray fell on the coast with cold air, the sea turned subtly gray. The cold waves shattere against the shore, bringing nothing but sands, and it awakened my toes with a vivid sense. All the noise surrounding me seemed to disappear for a moment in infinite space.

I walked along an endless stretch of coastline. Where only the sound of waves can reach my ears, the foggy sea visible in the distance has become a watercolor landscape. A person walking a dog and a sandy beach showing erosion and sedimentation caused by waves were also became a watercolor.

While walking for a while, I came across a pretty pebble. A heart that everyone would like. When did someone make such a pretty shape? I only watched it with my eyes because I knew that it would not be a heart shape if I took it out by hand. For a moment, the rushing waves covered it with sand in an instant as if they were jealous, leaving no trace.

우리 생도 이와 다를 게 없지. 찬란했거나 기억조차 하기 싫었던 과거라고 해도 다시 오지 않을 것이다. 세월이 순식간에 흘러간다는 것을 예순이 지난 요즘에 알았으니…. 오늘이 내 생에 가장 젊은 날이고, 지금이 가장 소중한 시간임을 잊지 말아야지.

5월의 따스한 햇살이 구름을 젖히며 나오자 희미했던 바다는 말끔하게 세수하고 나온 아이처럼 맑아졌다. 바다도 하늘도 온통 푸른 도화지가 되었다.

Our lives are no different. Even if it was a past that was brilliant and colorful or I didn't even want to remember, it wouldn't come back. Now that I'm in my sixties, I realize that time flies by in the blink of an eye···. I should not forget that today is the youngest day of my life, and this is the most precious time.

As the warm sunshine of May came out leaning against the clouds, the faint sea became clear like a child who washed her face cleanly. The sea and the sky turned into blue paper.

캐넌 비치

멀리 보이는 캐넌 비치를 향해 다시 차를 몰았다. 캐넌 비치는 '오리건 코스트'라고 불리는 북쪽 애스토리아(Astoria)에서 남쪽 브루킹스(Brookings)까지 이어진 585㎞ 해안선 중간에 있는 헤이스톡 바위(Haystack Rock)로 유명한 바닷가이다. 내셔널 지오그래픽이 선정한 세계에서 가장 아름다운 100곳 중 하나인데, 특히 일몰이 아름다워 사람들이 모여든다.

광안리나 해운대처럼 비치 중심에는 호텔을 비롯하여 주차장, 음식점, 기념품 가게, 우체국, 마트, 빵집 등 관광 인프라를 잘 갖추고 있었다.

안개가 모든 소음을 삼키고 바다는 은은한 회색으로 물들었다. 파도 소리는 멀리서 들려오는 속삭임처럼 잔잔했고, 촉촉한 모래 위로 부드럽게 밀려왔다 사라졌다. 거인의 그림자처럼 우뚝 솟은 헤이스톡 바위는 태곳적부터 그 자리를 지켜온 수호신 같았다.

Cannon Beach

I drove back towards Cannon Beach in the distance. Cannon Beach is a waterfront known for its Haystack Rock midway through the 585 kilometer coastline from northern Astoria to southern Brookings, called the Oregon Coast. It is one of the 100 most beautiful places in the world by National Geographic, especially the sunset is beautiful, attracting people.

Like Gwangalli and Haeundae, the center of the beach was well equipped with tourist infrastructure such as hotels, parking lots, restaurants, souvenir shops, post offices, marts, and bakeries.

The sea turned a subtle gray after mist swallowed all the noise. The sound of the waves was as calm as a whisper coming from a distance, gently pushed over the moist sand and disappeared. The Haystack Rock, which stands tall like the shadow of a giant, was like a guardian deity who has been there since ancient times.

파도가 부딪치는 바위 아래쪽은 제법 침식이 되었다. 깎인 그곳에는 도토리 키 재기를 하는 것처럼 홍합과 고동 등이 올망졸망 붙어있었다. 홍합보다 더 큰 몸집으로 다양한 색을 뽐내는 불가사리들이 징그러웠다. 그들도 조개류를 잡아먹으며 주어진 삶에 최선을 다하고 있는 것이겠지.

바위는 환경단체 봉사자들이 보호하고 있었는데 물이 빠지자 제한된 바위 주변을 걷도록 허락해 주었다. 바위의 숨결을 느끼기 위해서일까, 몇몇 사람들이 맨발로 거대한 바위 주변을 걸었다. 작은 돌들을 덮었던 이끼는 햇빛에 축 늘어져 다시 파도가 찾아줄 것을 기다렸다.

The bottom of the rock hit by the waves has become quite eroded. In the shaved place, mussels and thorns were attached as if they were measuring acorn height. The starfish, which are larger than mussels and show off various colors, were disgusting. They too are probably doing their best with the life they have been given, eating shellfish.

The rock was protected by volunteers from environmental groups, and when the water drained, the area was restricted and allowed to walk around the rock. Maybe to feel the rock's breath, some people walked around the huge rock barefoot. The moss, which covered the small stones, drooped in the sun and waited for the waves to return.

단단한 암벽은 새들의 숙소였다. 아침 일찍, 퍼핀도 날아다니는 것을 보았다고 누군가 귀띔해 주었다. 수많은 철새가 둥지를 틀고 부지런히 먹이를 나르며 새끼를 키우기에 바빴다. 작은 날개로 바람에 맞서 강인하게 날아다니던 철새의 모습에서 끈질긴 삶의 아름다움이 느껴졌다. 자식을 위해 희생하시는 부모님처럼, 새끼를 위해 먹이를 구하러 날아다니는 새들에게서 묘한 경외심마저 들었다.

새들의 울음소리는 안개를 타고 멀리 퍼져나가 바다의 고요함과 어우러졌다. 열심히 날았던 철새들이 날개를 바위에 내려놓고, 그들과 한 몸이 되어 쉬고 있었다. 웅크린 철새의 실루엣은 거대한 바위에 비해 작고 연약했다.

바위 주변에 물이 빠져 생긴 작은 웅덩이들이 반짝였다. 웅덩이 근처에서 파도가 밀려와 모래성이 허물어져도 아랑곳하지 않고 깔깔 웃는 아이들의 맑은 웃음소리가 들려왔다. 신기한 보물을 발견한 듯 예쁜 조개껍데기를 찾는 또 다른 가족에게서 소박하지만 따뜻한 행복이 묻어났다.

모든 풍경이 어우러져 캐넌 비치는 시간마저 느리게 흘러가는 듯한 평화로운 그림을 완성하였다. 그 안에 스며든 모든 존재는 자연과 하나 되어 숨 쉬고 있었다.

The rock wall was a place for birds. Someone tipped me off that they saw a puffin flying around early in the morning. Numerous migratory birds were busy nesting, diligently carrying food, and raising their young. The beauty of persistent life was felt in the image of migratory birds flying strong against the wind with small wings. Just like parents who sacrifice for their children, I felt a strange sense of awe at the birds that flew to find food for their chicks.

The birds' cries spread far and wide through the fog and blended with the stillness of the sea. The migratory birds that had been flying hard were resting their wings on the rock, becoming one with them. The silhouette of the curled migratory bird was small and fragile compared to the giant rock.

Small pools of water gleamed around the rocks. I heard the clear laughter of the children laughing regardless of the waves coming from near the puddle and the sand castle was torn down. Simple but warm happiness was buried in another family looking for a pretty shell as if they had discovered a mysterious treasure.

With all the scenery harmonizing, Canon Beach completed a peaceful picture that seemed to pass slowly even the time. All beings that permeated it were breathing as one with nature.

파웰 서점

점심을 간단히 먹고 차가 막히기 전에 포틀랜드로 돌아왔다. 포틀랜드의 대표 랜드마크인 파웰 서점에 들렀다. CNN이 정한 '세계 최고의 서점 1위'와 가디언즈 선정 '세계의 독립 서점 1위'를 차지할 정도로 유명한 서점이다. 거리 한 블록 전체가 다 서점 건물이라니! 규모가 꽤 컸다.

1971년부터 운영해 온 3층 건물의 서점에서는 새 책만 판매하는 것이 아니라 귀한 책도 구경할 수 있었다. 거대한 공간에 들어서는 순간, 시간은 묘하게 멈춰선 듯했다. 새 책과 헌책, 먼지 쌓인 고서와 빛바랜 절판본으로 빼곡한 책장 사이로, 알 수 없는 이야기의 향기가 가득 퍼져 나왔다.

Powell's Books

I had a quick lunch and came back to Portland before I got stuck in traffic. I stopped by Powell Bookstore, Portland's representative landmark. It is famous enough to rank No. 1 in the world's best bookstore by CNN and No. 1 in independent bookstores by Guardians. The whole block of the street is a bookstore building! It was quite large.

The three-story bookstore, which has been in operation since 1971, not only sells new books, but also offers valuable books. Between the bookshelves, which were filled with new and old books, dusty old volumes, and faded out-of-print editions, the scent of unknown stories permeated the air.

아이들에겐 미로 같은 통로를 헤치고 들어가서 숨겨진 보물을 찾듯 마주친 책 한 권이 그들의 상상력을 자극하고 무한한 세계를 선물할 것이다. 쿠사마 야요이, 반 고흐 같은 아티스트 카드나 수첩, 에코백, 머그컵 등 굿즈와 다양한 기념품과 양말, 인형 등을 갖춘 문화 성전이었다.

엄마가 책을 고르는 동안 어린이 코너에서 천진난만하게 노는 아이 둘은 얼마나 즐겁고 행복한 시간일까. 커피 한 잔을 시켜 종일 공짜로 책을 읽다가, 서점 안 꽃집에 들러 꽃 한 다발 사서 집으로 돌아간다면 가족 모두에게 말할 수 없는 기쁨이겠지.

지친 발걸음으로 서점을 나서는 순간에도 강렬하고 멋진 서점의 기억들이 나의 뇌리에 머물렀다.

For children, a book they encountered was like a hidden treasure, found after pushing through maze-like passages will stimulate their imagination and present an infinite world. It was a cultural temple with artist cards such as Yayoi Kusama and Van Gogh, goods such as notebooks, eco-bags, mugs, and various souvenirs, socks, and dolls.

What a fun and happy time it would be for two children to play innocent in the children's section while their mother chooses a book! If you order a cup of coffee and read a book for free all day, and then stop by the flower shop in the bookstore and buy a bunch of flowers and go home, it's a joy you can't tell your family.

Even when I left the bookstore with tired steps, the memories of the intense and wonderful bookstore remained in my mind.

스프링 가든

다음 날, 아침 식사 후 먼저 스프링 가든을 찾았다. 정식 명칭은 크리스털 스프링스 로도덴드론 가든이다. 미국 진달래학회 포틀랜드 지부에서 1950년에 진달래를 전시하기 위한 정원을 설립하고자 하였다.

셰익스피어 반도라고 불렸던 불모지였던 곳을 선정하고, 관리하다가 1951년에 크리스털 스프링스 국립 시험 정원으로 인정받았다. 신시아 진달래 두 그루로 시작한 정원은 자원봉사자와 관심 있는 분들의 후원으로 지금은 2,500그루가 넘는 진달래와 철쭉의 명소로 알려졌다.

1964년에 크리스털 스프링스 진달래 정원으로 이름이 바뀌었다. 포틀랜드의 조경 건축가인 윌리스 K. 헌팅턴이 1977년에 설계하였고, 후드 산과 애덤스 산에서 채취한 돌로 폭포 등 구조물을 설치하였다. 현재는 장애인을 위한 산책로까지 겸비하고 있었다.

호수와 철쭉이 유명하다는데 '얼마나 대단하겠어'라는 시니컬한 마음으로 방문하였다. 인공호수, 연못, 폭포 등이 있는 정원에는 다양한 수목들이 큰 키를 자랑하였다.

입장하면 풋풋한 흙 내음과 습기를 머금은 공기, 향긋한 꽃 내음이 발길을 이끌어 주었다. 오른쪽 아래로 내려가면 작은 연못을 메인으로 주변이 조성되었다. 연못 끝 지점에는 많은 수생식물이 자라고 있어서 오리나 철새들의 서식지가 되어주었다.

Springs Garden

Next day after breakfast, I went to Spring Garden first. The official name is Crystal Springs Roadodendron Garden. The Portland branch of the American Azalea Society wanted to establish a garden for displaying azaleas in 1950.

After selecting and managing a barren place called the Shakespeare Peninsula, it was recognized as the Crystal Springs National Testing Garden in 1951. The garden, which started with two Cynthia azaleas, is now known as a famous spot for more than 2,500 Rhododendron and royal azaleas with the support of volunteers and interested people.

It was renamed the Crystal Springs Azalea Garden in 1964. It was designed in 1977 by Portland landscape architect Wallace K. Huntington and installed structures such as stone waterfalls collected from Mount Hood and Mount Adams. It now even has a walkway for the disabled.

I visited the lake and royal azaleas with a cynical mind, thinking how great it must be. The garden, which included an artificial lake, pond, and waterfall, boasted a variety of tall trees.

When I entered, the smell of fresh soil, moist air, and fragrant flowers led me to visit. I go down to the lower right, the surroundings were created with a small pond as the main. At the end of the pond, many aquatic plants were growing, making it a habitat for ducks and migratory birds.

흐렸던 날씨에 때마침 빛이 찾아들어 반영을 찍는 사람들의 움직임이 빨라졌다. 연못 속에 길게 늘어진 수양버들과 키 큰 나무 그림자도 가끔 부는 바람에 함께 춤을 추었다. 사람은 멋진 피사체가 되어 물에 비친 식물과 함께 한 폭의 그림처럼 앵글에 담겼다.

정원을 걷는 내내 진달래와 철쭉, 만병초 등 같은 듯 다른 모습과 여러 가지 색을 지닌 아름다운 꽃들이 눈길을 끌었다. 강렬한 붉은색, 부드러운 분홍, 신비스러운 자줏빛, 고고한 흰색, 보기 드문 노란색까지 뒤섞여 시샘하듯 커다란 꽃송이를 뽐내었다.

2,500여 그루라는 숫자는 그저 많은 꽃이 아니었다. 정원을 가꾼 수많은 이들의 손길과 시간이 응축된 결과물이었다. 꽃잎에서 그들의 노력과 흔적이 호수의 잔물결처럼 반짝거렸다. 이곳을 찾는 사람들에게 꽃의 아름다움만 보여주는 것이 아니라 가슴 깊이 차오르는 뭉클함도 선물하였다.

The sunshin came in just in time in the cloudy weather, and the movement of people taking the reflection accelerated. Sometimes when the wind blew, the long willows and the shadows of tall trees in the pond also danced together. A person becomes a wonderful subject and is captured in an angle like a picture with a plant reflected in the water.

Throughout the walk through the garden, beautiful flowers with look alike yet different appearances and various colors such as Korean Rhododendron, Royal Azaleas, and Alpine rhododendron caught my eye. They showed off large flowers as if they were jealous, mixed with intense red, soft pink, mysterious purple, noble white, and rare yellow.

The number 2,500 wasn't just a lot of flowers. It was the result of condensation of the works and time of many people who grew the garden. On the petals, their efforts and traces glistened like ripples in the lake. It not only showed the beauty of flowers to those who visited this place, but also presented the heart-deep emotion.

호수에서는 하얀 물길이 솟아올라 마치 보트의 돛을 연상시켰다. 푸른색의 수국도 곳곳에서 살며시 고개를 내밀었다. 산책 코스를 따라가니 바로 옆에 있는 골프장까지도 정원인 양 착각에 빠져서 훨씬 넓어 보였다.

비가 내리기 시작하였다. 꽃 색에 반하고 향기에 취해 느려진 발걸음을 재촉해서 차로 돌아왔다.

A white waterway rose from the lake, reminiscent of the sails of a boat. The blue hydrangeas also gently raised their heads from all over the place. I followed the walking path, even the golf course next door looked much wider because I was mistaken for a garden.

It began to rain. In love with the color of the flowers, drunk on the scent, I hurried my slow steps back to the car.

트롤 공원

다음 목적지는 트롤(Troll) 공원이었다. 트롤은 북유럽 신화나 전설에 나오는 마술을 부리는 거인을 뜻한다. 시애틀이나 포틀랜드에는 북유럽에서 이주해 온 사람들이 많은지, 시내를 다니면서 모양이 조금씩 다른 귀여운 트롤을 보았다.

공원은 꽤 넓었고, 북유럽 형식으로 지어진 작은 집도 몇 채 있었다. 커다란 트롤이 집 안을 들여다보고 있는 모습이 귀엽기도 하고, 우습기도 하였다. 내가 집 안에 들어가 트롤을 쳐다보며 사진을 찍으니 그와 대화를 하는 것처럼 느껴졌다.

트롤 공원은 스테이너 가족의 땅이었으나 현재 거주하는 손자가 나라에 기증한 상태였다. 자원봉사자들 역시 북유럽에서 온 후손으로 일주일에 한 번씩 모여 나이 드신 주인장 일을 도와주거나 그 집을 수리하면서 하루를 보낸다고 하였다.

Troll Park

The next destination was Troll Park. A troll is a giant who performs magic in North Europe mythology or legends. There seemed to be many people who migrated from Northern Europe in Seattle or Portland. As I went around the city, I saw a cute troll with a slightly different shape.

The park was quite large, and there were a few small houses built in the Nordic style. It was cute and funny to see a large troll looking into the house. As I went inside the house, looked at the trolls and took pictures, it felt like I was talking to him.

The Troll Park was originally a Steiner family's property, but had been donated to the country by his grandson. Volunteers are also descendants from Northern Europe who gather once a week to help the elderly owner or spend the day repairing the house.

트롤을 구경하고 나서 봉사자 한 분이 주인 허락을 받아 집 안을 구경시켜 주었다. 90살쯤으로 보이는 집주인 할아버지는 조상에 대한 자부심이 상당했다.

스웨덴에서 이주해 온 그의 조상은 부유한 가문이었다. 당시 가져온 가구를 비롯한 그릇, 액자, 괘종시계, 카펫, 전통 의상 등에서 품격이 드러났다. 낡은 가족사진, 소품 한 점 한 점이 소중하게 보였다.

오래된 피아노에 앉아 내 고향 부산과 지금 사는 제주를 떠올리며 「고향의 봄」을 연주하였다. 세계 공통 언어인 노래를 들으며 그분들도 그 순간에는 스웨덴을 그리워하는 추억에 빠져들지 않았을까.

After watching the trolls, a volunteer showed me around the house with the owner's permission. The elderly landlord. who looked about 90 years old, had considerable pride in his ancestors.

His ancestors, who immigrated from Sweden, were from a wealthy family. Dignity was revealed in the furniture, bowls, frames, wall clocks, carpets and traditional clothes that he brought at the time. Old family photographs and props seemed precious.

Sitting on an old piano, I played 「Spring of Hometown」, recalling my hometown of Busan and Jeju Island, where I live now. Listening to the song, which is a common language in the world, wouldn't they have fallen into memories of missing Sweden at that moment?

대가족의 저녁 식사

집으로 돌아와 저녁을 준비하였다. 어제는 둘째 코디(Cody)랑 결혼할 여성, 레이첼이 와서 함께 저녁을 먹었다. 레이첼은 한국 출신 입양아였다. 어제는 그녀가 한국 음식을 종종 요리할 정도로 좋아한다고 하여서 불고기와 잡채를 만들었다.

어제와 같은 음식을 다시 대접할 수가 없어서 오늘은 레이첼이 먹고 싶다는 음식, 처음으로 김말이 튀김에 도전하였다. 그녀가 몇 가지 재료를 가져왔고, 우리도 집으로 오는 길에 마트에서 필요한 재료를 사 왔다.

사 먹기만 했던 음식이라 여러 사이트를 검색해서 만드는 방법을 찾았다. 잔손이 가는 요리였지만 후배와 레이첼이 맡아서 했는데, 아들들도 간간이 도와주어 명절 음식을 만드는 것처럼 즐거웠다.

나는 간장 양념 찜닭을 메인으로 준비하면서 가지전을 부쳤다. 우리 음식을 소개할 수 있다는 생각에 정성을 다하였다. 첫째 아들과 파트너까지 방문하여 모두 8인분 요리를 준비하니 시간이 생각보다 많이 걸렸다.

A large family's dinner

I returned home and prepared dinner. Yesterday, Rachel who was going to marry Cody came and had dinner together. Rachel was a Korean adoptee. Yesterday, I made bulgogi and japchae since she said she likes Korean food so much that she cooks it often.

I couldn't serve the same food as yesterday again, so I tried the food that Rachel wanted to eat today, fried seaweed roll for the first time. She brought some ingredients, and we also bought the ingredients we needed at the market on our way home.

I searched several sites and found a way to make it because it was a food I only bought. It was a fine dish, but my juniors and Rachel were in charge of it, and Cody also helped them occasionally and enjoyed making holiday food.

I prepared soy sauce marinated steamed chicken as the main dish and fried eggplant pancakes. I put my heart and soul into introducing our food. Lynn's first son and partner visited and prepared a dish for 8 people. It took more time to cook than I thought.

한국서 들고 온 양념 김을 내어 밥을 싸서 먹는 것까지 알려주었다. 밥을 김에 싸서 먹는 것은 K 드라마나 영화를 통해 널리 알려져서 둘째 부부는 이미 알고 있었다. 몇 년 전보다 한국 문화가 널리 확산되고 있음을 피부로 느꼈다.

린과 테리는 오랜만에 아들과 며느리까지 모여 음식을 함께 먹으니 그지없이 행복해 보였다. 한국 음식에 이미 맛 들인 코디와 레이첼은 말할 것도 없고, 첫째 아들 커플도 맛있다고 미소를 지었다. 모두 맛있게 잘 먹어주니 나는 진짜 요리사가 된 기분이었다.

식사 후, 코디는 아버지 어깨와 발 마사지를 비롯하여 엄마의 푸념도 다정하게 들어주었다. 막내는 태어날 때부터 다른가. 성인이 되어도 귀여운 짓을 하는 것이 막내의 역할이지 싶다. 코디와 비교하니 나는 부모님께 살갑게 대하지 못한, 무뚝뚝한 막내딸이었다.

I taught them how to wrap rice with seasoned seaweed from Korea. Cody and Rachel they already knew that rice wrapped in seaweed was widely known through K-dramas and movies. I felt that Korean culture was spreading more widely than it had in a few years.

Lynn and Terry looked very happy to be eating together with their son and daughter-in-law after such a long time. Not to mention Cody and Rachel, who have already tasted Korean food, the first son couple also smiled that it was delicious. Everyone ate well, so I felt like a real chef.

After the meal, Cody gently listened to her mother's complaints, including his father's shoulder and foot massage. Is the youngest different from birth? I think it is the role of the youngest to do something cute even when he becomes an adult. Compared to Cody, I was the blunt youngest daughter who couldn't be nice to my parents.

펄루스

Palouse

고요 속에서 터져 나온 빛의 폭포

밀밭이 있는 펄루스까지 570여 킬로미터, 6시간이 걸린다. 도심을 벗어나 컬럼비아 리버 고속도로에 들어서니 캐나다서 시작된 컬럼비아강이 펼쳐졌다. 하늘보다 더 푸른 색의 강은 대관식에 참여하는 병정들처럼 웅장하게 흘렀다. 멈춘 듯 유유히 흐르는 강 오른쪽으로 도로와 철로가 나 있었다.

50분쯤 걸려 린이 추천해 준 멀트노마(Multnomah) 폭포에 도착하였다. 포틀랜드 시내에서도 멀지 않고, 고속도로 옆에 있어서 방문하기 쉬운 곳이었다. 미국에서 두 번째로 높은 약 620피트(190m)의 2단 폭포로, 영화 「트와일라잇」 촬영지로 알려져서 유명세를 탔던 곳이다.

폭포 입구 휴게소는 일찍 온 사람들로 붐벼서 우리는 곧장 폭포로 향하였다. 양쪽 산에 안긴 폭포는 새벽 공기를 머금은 채, 깊은 잠에 빠져있었다. 폭포는 압도적인 소리로만으로 자신의 존재감을 나타내었다. 웅장한 물소리가 내 심장을 때리는 동안 나는 고개를 들어 폭포 꼭대기 너머를 응시하였다. 무언가 터져 나올 듯한 고요 속에는 오직 자연의 날것 그대로의 숨결만이 가득하였다.

Waterfalls of Light from the Silence

It takes about 570 kilometers and 6 hours to get to Palouse, where there is a wheat field. The Columbia River, which started in Canada, flowed as I leaved the city and entered the Columbia River Expressway. The river, bluer than the sky, flowed majestically like soldiers participating in the coronation. There were roads and railways on the right side of the river, which flows leisurely as if it looks stopped.

It took about 50 minutes to arrive at Multnomah Falls, which Lynn recommended. It was not far from downtown Portland, so it was easy to visit because it was next to the highway. It is the second-highest two-stage waterfall in the United States, about 620 feet (190 meters), and was famous for being known as the filming location of the movie 「Twilight」.

The resturant at the entrance of the waterfall was crowded with early visitors, so we headed straight for the waterfall. The waterfall on both sides of the mountain was in deep sleep, with the dawn air in it. The waterfall only expressed its presence with an overwhelming sound. I looked up and stared over the top of the waterfall while the magnificent sound of water hit my heart. In the silence that seemed to burst something, there was only a natural, raw breath.

시간은 더디게 흐르는 듯했다. 오전 10시쯤이었을까, 약속이라도 한 듯 산 정상에서 한 줄기 빛이 비쳤다. 숨죽이며 기다리던 태양이 드디어 장막을 걷어내기 시작하였다. 망설이듯 조심스레 내민 얼굴이 이내 찬란한 황금빛으로 반짝였다.

빛이 닿는 순간, 칙칙했던 폭포는 마법처럼 생동감이 넘쳤다. 쏟아져 내리는 물줄기는 은빛 비늘처럼 반짝였다. 어둠 속에 갇혀 있던 웅장한 물소리는 빛과 함께 춤추는 교향곡이 되어 계곡을 가득 메웠다. 그 순간을 놓치지 않으려고 카메라 셔터를 눌렀다. 찰나의 미학, 어둠과 빛, 소리와 침묵이 완벽한 조화를 이루는 기적 같은 순간을 붙잡으려는 몸부림이었다.

폭포 중간에 있는 다리까지 10분, 카메라와 삼각대를 메고 가는 길이 쉽지 않았지만 멋진 풍광을 기대하니 콧노래가 나왔다. 물줄기와 폭포 주변이 강한 빛으로 제대로 나오지 않았으면 어쩌나 걱정했는데 시도한 장노출이 그런대로 성공하였다.

꼭대기까지 다녀오는 사람도 있었으나 나는 떨어지는 물소리에 취해 한참 동안 다리 가운데 서 있었다. 저 물은 어디서 와서 어디까지 흘러갈까.

사진으로 다 담을 수 없는, 짧지만 강렬했던 한 줄기 빛의 등장. 내 눈과 귀, 나의 마음속에는 오월의 멀트노마가 선물한 한 편의 드라마가 선명하게 새겨졌다. 웅장한 폭포는 내 기억 속에 남아 영원히 흐를 것이다.

Time seemed to be running slowly. Perhaps it was around 10 a.m., a ray of light shone from the top of the mountain as if it had been promised. The sun, which had been waiting with bated breath, finally began to clear the shroud. As if hesitating, the sun, which was released carefully, soon glistened with brilliant gold.

The moment the light hit, the once dull waterfall magically burst into life. The cascading water sparkled like silver scales. The magnificent sound of water trapped in the dark became a symphony dancing with light and filled the valley. I pressed the camera shutter not to miss the moment. It was a struggle to seize a miraculous moment in which the instant aesthetic, darkness and light, sound and silence were in perfect harmony.

It was not easy to get to the bridge in the middle of the waterfall for 10 minutes, carrying a camera and a tripod, but I hummed when I expected a wonderful view. I was worried about what if the water stream and the area around the waterfall did not come out properly with strong light, but the intestinal exposure I tried was successful.

Some people came all the way to the top, but I stood in the middle of the bridge for a long time, drunk by the sound of falling water. Where will that water come from and how far will it flow?

The appearance of a short but intense ray of light that cannot be captured by photography. A drama presented by May's Multnomah was clearly etched in my eyes and ears also in my heart. The magnificent waterfall will remain in my memory and flow forever.

로웨나 크레스트

폭포를 빠져나오니 바로 84번 고속도로와 연결되었다. 도로 왼쪽은 컬럼비아강이, 오른쪽은 절벽이 계속해서 이어졌다. 산을 깎아 도로를 만들었기에 볼 수 있는 현상이었다. 일직선 도로가 아닌 구불구불한 도로를 보니 본래 모습을 살리려고 정부에서 노력했다는 것을 알 수 있었다. 자연스러워 보이는 절벽에 나타난 지층은 그랜드캐니언의 일부 같았다. 컬럼비아강 주변의 협곡은 화산 활동과 수백만 년에 걸쳐 현무암이 침식되면서 생겨난 것인데 길가에 보이는 절벽은 협곡의 연장선이었다.

도로표지판에서 강 주변에는 크고 작은 폭포들과 관광지가 있다고 알려주었지만 우리는 갈 길이 멀어서 모두 지나쳤다. 인류 문명의 발생지가 강 유역에서 시작된 것처럼 강 건너편에는 가끔 마을이 있었고, 다리도 보였다.

강을 건너가서 마을을 구경하고 싶었으나 컬럼비아강을 건널 수 있는 다리는 두 시간을 달려서 겨우 하나가 나타났다. 이에 비하면 우리나라는 작은 영토임에도 불구하고 강마다 많은 다리가 놓여서 마을 간의 왕래가 얼마나 편한지.

Rowena Crest

As soon as I left the waterfall, I was connected to Highway 84. The Columbia River continued on the left side of the road, and the cliff continued on the right side. It was a phenomenon that could be seen because the road was built by cutting the mountain. Looking at the winding road rather than the straight road, it can be seen that the government tried to save its original natural appearance. The strata that appeared on the natural-looking cliffs were like part of the Grand Canyon. The canyon around the Columbia River was created by volcanic activity and the erosion of basalt over millions of years, and the cliff seen on the side of the road was an extension of the canyon.

The road sign informed us that there are large or small waterfalls and tourist attractions around the river, but we all passed because we had a long way to go. Just as the birthplace of human civilization began in the river basin, there were occasional villages across the river, and bridges were visible.

I wanted to go across the river and see the village, but one bridge appeared after two hours of driving across the Columbia River. Compared to this, even though Korea is a small territory, there are many bridges in each river, so it is easy to go and go between villages.

마이어 주립공원과 컬럼비아강의 멋진 협곡의 경치를 제대로 즐기라고 풍경 도로의 목적으로 건설된 로웨나 크레스트 뷰포인트(Rowena Crest View Point)로 차를 몰았다. 자전거를 타는 분들이 비지땀을 쏟으며, 모터바이크족들이 웅장한 엔진 소리를 내며 경사진 도로를 올라올 정도로 가치가 넘치는 곳이었다.

안전상의 이유로 만들어둔 담 위에 올라앉았다. 막힘없는 하늘과 끝없는 강물에 한 톨의 답답한 마음도 다 씻겨나가는 기분이었다. 굽이굽이 올라온 고도 위에서 내려다본 풍경은 그야말로 대자연이 펼쳐놓은 거대한 풍경화였다.

원근감이 무엇인지 제대로 보여주는 듯 컬럼비아 강줄기는 끝없이 이어졌다. 마치 세상의 깊이를 알려주려는 듯 강물은 유유히 흐르며, 아득히 먼 지평선 속으로 사라져 가는 듯했다.

I drove to Rowena Crest View Point, which was built for the purpose of a landscape road, to enjoy the views of Meyer State Park and the magnificent canyon of the Columbia River. It was a place of such value that cyclists were sweating, and motorbikes climbed the sloping road with a magnificent engine sound.

I sat on a wall made for safety reasons. I felt as if every single pent-up feeling in my heart was being washed away by the unobstructed sky and endless river. The scenery viewed from the winding elevation was truly a huge landscape of Mother Nature.

As if to properly show what perspective is, the Columbia River continued endlessly. The river flowed slowly as if to reveal the depth of the world, it seemed to be disappearing into the distant horizon.

마치 레고 장난감으로 만든 것처럼, 강 건너에 있는 집들과 마을과 마을을 잇는 교각 등이 손톱만큼 작았다. 발아래 도로를 오가는 자동차들은 태엽을 감은 작은 모형들이 움직이는 듯이 꼬물거렸다.

생전 처음으로 60량이 넘는 화물 기차를 보았다. 긴 꼬리를 몰고 느릿느릿 지나가는 기차는 대자연 속에 사는 작은 존재들의 끈질긴 여정처럼 보였다. 강 한편에 자리한 고요한 인공호수에 내려앉은 햇살은 유독 반짝였다. 호수는 거대한 그림에 숨결을 불어넣는 화룡점정이 되었다.

혼자 보기 너무 아까운 풍광이었다. 누군가에게 보여주기 위해 뷰포인트를 한 바퀴 돌면서 동영상을 찍었다. 이곳에서 출발할 수 있는 트레킹 코스도 있는지 등산 차림의 부부가 산에서 걸어왔다. 들판에는 여기저기서 피어난 봄꽃 야생화가 제각각 아름다움을 뽐내었다. 멀리 레이니어산 꼭대기의 눈 쌓인 모습이 보였다.

멋진 뷰를 가진 자연 레스토랑, 로웨나 크레스트 뷰포인트에서 먹은 점심은 꿀맛이었다.

As if they were made from Lego toys, the houses across the river and the piers connecting the village to the village were as small as fingernails. Cars moving along the road under my feet were wriggling as if wind-up small models were moving around.

I saw more than 60 freight trains for the first time in my life. The train, slowly passing by with its long tail, seemed like the tenacious journey of small beings living in the great outdoors. The sunlight on the quiet artificial lake on the one side of the river was particularly shiny. The lake became the final touch that infuse the grand scene with life.

It was such a waste of scenery to see alone. I took a video around the viewpoints to show someone. A couple dressed in hiking walked from the mountain to see if there was a tracking course that could start from here. In the field, each spring flower blooming here and there showed off its beauty. In the distance, the snow-covered peak of Mount Rainier was visible.

The lunch at the Rowena Crest View Point, a natural restaurant with a nice view, was delicious.

뷰 좋은 숙소

강을 따라 고속도로는 계속 이어졌다. 컬럼비아강이 미 서부 개척에서 커다란 역할을 했음이 분명했다. 간간이 나타난 작은 공장과 마을이 강을 토대로 발전을 거듭하는 중이었다. 멀리 보이는 풍력 발전기는 전기 생산에 한몫하겠지.

84번 고속도로에서 벗어나 내륙으로 들어서니 그렇게 보고 싶었던 밀밭이 드러났다. 40분 이상 끝없이 이어졌다. 콜팩스 마을에서 주유하고, 슈퍼마켓에서 며칠 동안 먹을 장을 보았다.

에어비앤비 숙소에 도착하니 다행히 주인장이 있었다. 부족한 조리 기구를 빌리고, 궁금한 사항을 질문하였다. 숙소는 주인이 사는 집 차고 옆을 연결하며 현대식으로 새로 지은 고급 펜션 같은 2층이었다. 1층에 넓은 공간에 화장실이 있었고, 2층에 침실과 간이 부엌이 있어서 머무는 동안 멋진 뷰를 실컷 즐겼다. 한적하고, 제법 높은 지역에 있어서 별 찍기에 좋을 듯했다.

A room with a nice view

The highway continued along the river. It was obvious that the Columbia River played a major role in the development of the American West. Small factories and villages that appeared here and there were developing along the river. Wind turbines in the distance will contribute to electricity production.

Entering inland from Highway 84 revealed the wheat field that I wanted to see so much. The wheat field lasted for more than 40 minutes. I refuelled in the town of Colfax, and went grocery shopping for a few days at the supermarket.

Fortunately, when I arrived at Airbnb accommodation, there was an owner. I borrowed insufficient cooking utensils and asked questions. The accommodation was a two-story building, like a luxury pension newly built in a modern style, connecting next to the garage of the house where the owner lived. The first floor had a bathroom in a large space, and the second floor had a bedroom and a kitchenette, so I enjoyed the wonderful view during my stay. It was quiet and in a fairly high area, so it seemed good for shooting stars.

하나밖에 없는 화구에 밥과 된장국을 차례대로 요리하고, 야채볶음까지 만들어 늦은 저녁을 먹었다. 아래층 공간에다 짐을 풀었더니 필요한 물건을 챙기느라 오르락내리락 자연스럽게 운동이 되었다.

9시쯤 밖으로 나오니 이미 일몰이 끝났으나 불그스름한 하늘을 만났다. 낮 동안 흐렸던 날씨에 보상이라도 해주듯 깜깜한 밤하늘에 별이 쏟아졌다. 오랜만에 동심으로 돌아가 별 헤는 밤을 즐겼다.

I made rice and soybean paste soup in the only fire pit, and cooked stir-fried vegetables in order, so I had a late dinner. When I unpacked my luggage in the space downstairs, I went up and down to pack what I needed, so I naturally became an exercise.

When I came out around 9 o'clock, the sunset was already over, but I met the reddish sky. Stars poured into the dark night sky as if compensating for the cloudy weather during the day. After a long time, I went back to my childhood and enjoyed the night of counting stars.

펄루스 평원에 반하다

드디어 밀밭 풍경을 찍으러 가는 날이다. 날씨까지 화창해서 사진 찍기 더없이 좋은 날이었다. 스텝토, 콜팩스, 풀먼, 펄루스에 걸친 광대한 평원을 합쳐서 펄루스 밀밭이라 부른다. 인터넷에 올라온 사진들은 숙소에서 자동차로 30분 정도 떨어진 스텝토 뷰트(Steptoe Butte) 정상에서 찍은 것들이다.

숙소에서 스텝토 뷰트까지 가는 길은 두 가지였다. 다녀온 후에 알게 된 195도로는 비교적 포장이 잘되어 있었으나 내비게이션은 다른 길로 우리를 안내하였다. 안내된 길이 가까운 거리였을지는 몰라도, 비포장의 자갈길이었고, 질퍽거려서 조심스럽게 운전해야만 했다.

펄루스의 심장부를 가로지르는 초록 물결을 꿈꾸며 도착한 스텝토 뷰트, 운명의 장난처럼 길은 봉쇄되어 있었다. 문 닫힌 입구에서 한껏 부푼 나의 기대도 닫혀버렸다. 애초에 편리한 길이 대자연의 섭리 앞에서는 무의미했으리라. 한국서 여기까지 어떻게 왔는데…. 포기하기에는 너무 억울했다. 자동차를 입구에 두고 후배와 걸어 올라가기로 하였다. 걸어서 스텝토 뷰트까지 올라간 사람은 우리뿐이라 생각하니 피식 웃음이 나왔다.

Fall in love with the plains of Palouse

Finally, it's the day to take pictures of the wheat fields. It was a great day to take pictures because the weather was sunny and clear. The vast plains spanning Steptoe, Colfax, Pullman and Palouse are collectively called Palouse wheat fields. The photos posted on the Internet were taken at the top of of Mount Steptoe Butte, about a 30-minute drive from the accommodation.

There were two ways to get to Steptoe Butte from the accommodation. I found out after seeing that road 195 was relatively well paved, but the navigation led us to a different path. Although the route indicated was a short distance, it was an unpaved gravel road and muddy, so I had to drive carefully.

Steptoe Butte, I arrived dreaming of a green wave across the heart of Palouse, the road was blocked like a trick of fate. My expectations at the door-closed entrance were closed. In the first place, a convenient path would have been meaningless in front of Mother Nature's providence. How did I get here from Korea···. It was too unfair to give up, so I decided to leave the car at the entrance and walk up with my junior. When I thought we might be the only ones walking up to Steptoe Butte, I laughed.

빤히 보이는 산 정상이 가깝게 보였다. 자동차 도로인 데다 산모퉁이 돌아 뒤쪽이 보이지 않으니 얼마나 걸릴지 예측 불가였다. 한 시간이면 정상에 오를 수 있다고 생각하고, 오름을 올랐던 경험을 살려 빤히 보이는 정상을 향해 걸었다.

지름길은 밀밭을 가로질러 가야 하는데…. 밀밭 가운데로 밟고 가면 농부에게 피해를 줄 것 같아서 가장자리로 걸었다. 밀밭 언저리는 예상보다 훨씬 더 거칠었다. 처음 자갈길은 시작에 불과하였다. 밀밭으로 진입하는 들판에 선 큰 키의 도깨비바늘은 침입자를 지키는 파수꾼처럼 나의 옷자락을 붙잡으며 발걸음을 방해하였다. 내 키를 넘는 억새들은 사납게 제 몸을 휘저으며 나아가려는 우리를 방해하였다.

The peak of the mountain looked close. It was impossible to predict how long it would take because it was an vehicle road and the back was not visible around the corner. I thought I would be able to reach the top in an hour, and I walked toward the summit that I could see clearly using my experience of climbing the Oreum.

The shortcut is to cross the wheat field···. I walked to the edge because I thought it would be too damaging to the farmer if I stepped in the middle of the wheat field. The edge of the wheat field was much rougher than expected. The first gravel road was just the beginning. Standing in the field entering the wheat field, the tall goblin needle held me by the hem of my clothes like a watchman guarding the intruder and interfered with my steps. The silver grasses over my height interfered with us trying to move on, stirring their bodies violently.

누구든 가 보지 않은 길은 모르는 법이다. 한 치 앞을 예측할 수 없는 인생길도 마찬가지다. 평탄하게 보였던 길 웅덩이에 발이 젖기도 하고, 뾰족한 돌부리에 걸려 넘어지기도 한다. 때로는 외나무다리에서 원수를 만나기도 하고, 자칫하면 추락할 낭떠러지도 만난다. 사람은 지혜와 용기로 어려움을 헤쳐 나갈 능력이 있기에 묵묵히 주어진 길을 걸어간다.

그저 초록으로 보이던 산줄기는 가까이 다가갈수록 예상치 못한 민낯을 드러내었다. 푹 꺼진 땅과 사슴을 막을 요령으로 심은 가시나무, 이름 모를 잡목들과 덩굴이 거친 생명력으로 엉켜 있었다. 이 길은 단순한 산책로가 아닌 자연의 경고이자 도전자에게 주어지는 통과의례 같았다.

조금 오르다 간식을 먹으며 잠시 쉬었다. 고된 발걸음 끝에는 감탄사가 절로 터져 나오는 보상이 기다리고 있었다. 이름 모를 들꽃들은 저마다 고운 자태를 뽐내며 보석처럼 빛을 발했다. 고운 색으로 곤충은 물론 우리를 현혹시켰다. 바람은 지휘자였다. 구름이 흘러가는 속도에 맞추어 밀밭은 군무를 추었다. 능선을 따라 파도처럼 출렁이는 밀밭은 거친 숨결을 내쉬며 나를 압도하였다. 수확이 끝난 자리에서는 고스란히 드러난 누런 황토가 밭의 질감을 더욱 생생하게 드러내었다.

No one knows the way that they haven't been to. The same goes for life paths that cannot be predicted an inch ahead. We get our feet wet in puddles on the road that looked flat, and we also trip over a pointed stone. Sometimes we meet the enemy on a single tree bridge, and sometimes we meet a cliff that will fall. People walk silently on the given path because they have the ability to overcome difficulties with wisdom and courage.

The mountain range, which looked just green, revealed an unexpected bare face as it got closer. The ground that had been turned off, the thorn trees planted as a trick to prevent deer, and the unnamed weeds and vines were tangled with wild vitality. This road was not just a trail, but a warning from nature and a rite of passage given to the challenger.

I took a break while eating a snack as I climbed a little. At the end of the hard steps, there was a reward for exclamations. The unnamed wild flowers showed off their beautiful appearance and shone like jewels. They misled us as well as insects by their fine colors. Wind was a conductor. The wheat field danced to the speed of the clouds. The wheat fields swaying like waves along the ridge overwhelmed me with a rough breath. At the end of the harvest, the yellow ocher revealed the texture of the field more vividly.

시야에 보이는 밀밭은 다채로운 색상으로 펴져있었다. 고도가 높아지면서 경사가 커지니 걸음이 느려졌다. 후배는 6부 능선에서 오르기를 포기하고 사진 찍기 놀이에 빠졌다. 나는 계속 올라 8부 능선, 차가 다니는 길에 닿았다.

입구에서 보았던 모습과 다른 밀밭 경치가 펼쳐졌다. 등산가들이 정상을 정복하려는 의지를 알 것 같았다. 꼭대기를 올려다보니 경사가 너무 가파르고 잡목이 많아서, 8부 능선에서 멈추고 사진과 영상 찍기에 몰두하였다.

뒤쪽을 제외하고 눈앞에 180도로 펼쳐진 밀밭 풍광에 할 말을 잃었다. 보이는 것은 밀밭뿐이었다. 프리즘으로 퍼진 듯 햇살이 비추니 구역을 달리하여 각양각색의 밀밭이 드러났다. 그라데이션으로 연결된 부드러운 곡선이 예사롭지 않았다. 그저 '경이롭다, 광활하다'라는 말밖에 나오지 않았다. 띄엄띄엄 보이는 집과 울타리로 둘러싼 나무 몇 그루가 밀밭 평원을 더욱 평화롭게 만들었다.

The wheat fields in sight were spread out in colorful colors. As the altitude increased, the slope increased and the steps slowed down. The junior gave up climbing on the sixth ridge and fell into a photo-taking game. I kept climbing and reaching the eight-part ridge, the road where the car was running.

The view of the wheat field was different from that seen at the entrance. I could understand the climbers' willingness to conquer the summit. When I looked up at the top, the slope was too steep and there were too many clumps, so I stopped at the 8th ridge and was immersed in taking pictures and videos.

Except for the back, I was lost for words in the 180-degree wheat field scenery in front of me. All I could see was a wheat field. As the sun shone as if it had spread through a prism, various wheat fields were revealed by varying areas. The smooth curve connected by the gradation was not unusual. All I could say was, "It's marvelous, it's vast." Floating houses and a few trees surrounded by hedges made the wheat plain more peaceful.

하늘은 펄루스의 빛깔을 만드는 팔레트였다. 떠다니는 구름 무리와 쏟아지는 햇살의 방향에 따라 밀밭은 끝없이 옷을 갈아입었다. 가까운 곳은 싱그러운 초록으로, 때로는 푸른빛이 감도는 바다처럼, 멀리 아스라이 드리워진 안개와 겹치는 곳은 몽환적인 보랏빛으로 시선을 사로잡았다. 이 모든 빛깔의 향연은 살아 숨 쉬는 대자연의 숨결이었고, 예측 불가한 아름다움의 극치였다.

펄루스에서의 여정은 단순히 멋진 풍경을 눈에 담는 것으로 끝나지 않았다. 육체의 고통을 감수하고 나서 온전히 느낄 수 있었던 대자연의 경이로움에 빠져들었다. 그 안에서 내가 얼마나 작고 미미한 존재인지 깨닫는 시간이었다. 펄루스 밀밭은 나에게 품격 있는 아름다움을 넘어 고통과 인내를 통해 얻을 수 있는 삶의 진한 풍미를 선물하였다.

The sky was the palette that created the color of the Palouse. By the direction of the floating clouds and the pouring sunlight, the wheat fields changed clothes endlessly. Nearby were fresh greenery, and on one side, like a blue sea, overlapping the fog dimly cast in the distance revealed a dreamy purple light. The feast of all these colors was the breath of living and breathing Mother Nature, and the height of unpredictable beauty.

The journey in Palouse was more than just to capture the wonderful scenery. After enduring the pain of the body, I fell into the wonder of Mother Nature that I could fully feel. It was a time to realize how small and insignificant I was in it. The Palouse wheat field presented me with a rich flavor of life that could be obtained through pain and perseverance beyond elegant beauty.

정신없이 밀밭 찍기에 몰두하다가 후배가 있는 곳으로 내려오니 강한 햇살에 구름이 뒷걸음을 쳤다. 이때를 놓칠 수 없어 단 컷으로 카메라 셔터를 눌렀다. 핸드폰을 조작하여 인터넷서 보았던 풍경을 따라 비슷한 색감이 나올 때까지 찍었다.

빗방울이 떨어지자 발걸음이 빨라졌다. 비 내릴 때 산에서 걸었던 경험을 알기에 비가 세차게 내리기 전에 서둘러서 내려왔다. 올라갈 때 2시간 걸린 거리를 40분 만에 내려왔다. 마음먹기에 따라서 뭐든지 가능한 인간의 무한한 잠재력에 스스로 흐뭇해하였다.

다시 동쪽으로 30분 정도 운전하여 카미악 뷰트(Kamiak Butte)에 도착했다. 약속이나 한 듯이 이곳도 출입을 막고 있었다. 다음 날 길에서 만난 분에게서 알게 된 사실인데 비가 많이 내려 약간의 산사태가 나서 당분간 출입을 막는다고 하였다. 안전에 얼마나 민감한 나라인지. 머무는 날이 한정된 우리는 가드 라인을 넘고 도로를 따라 정상까지 걸었다.

While I was busy photographing the wheat field, I came down to where my junior was, and the clouds stepped back in the strong sunlight. I couldn't miss this time, so I pressed the camera shutter with a single cut. I manipulated my phone and took pictures until similar colors came out along the scenery I saw on the Internet.

When the raindrops fell, my steps sped up. Knowing the experience of walking in the mountains when it rained, I hurried down before it rained hard. It took me two hours to go up, and I came down in 40 minutes. I was pleased with the infinite potential of human beings that could do anything depending on my mind.

I drove about half an hour east again and arrived at Kamiak Butte. This place was also blocked from entering as if it had been promised with the Steptoe Butte, I heard from a person I met on the road the next day, not long ago, it rained a lot and caused a little landslide, so it was blocked from entering for the time being. What a safety-sensitive country. With limited days to stay, we crossed the guard line and walked to the top along the road.

스텝토 뷰트에서 보았던 노란색이 이곳이었을까. 길가에는 해바라기를 닮은 뚱딴지 꽃과 금계국이 군집을 이루어 카메라를 유혹하였다. 두 꽃의 노란색은 부드럽고 따뜻해서 눈이 부시기보다 마음이 환해지는 색이었다. 노란 들판에 들어간 나는 한 송이 꽃이 되었다.

정상에 오르자 바람이 조용히 내 어깨를 감싸안았다. 자연이 온몸으로 숨 쉬는 듯 땅과 하늘 사이에 부드러운 호흡이 이어지고 있었다. 초록으로 지평선 끝까지 펼쳐진 밀밭은 바람에 몸을 맡겼다. 자라는 모습과 수확 후의 자국이 한 화면에 나란히 보였다.

스텝토 뷰트에서 바라보는 풍광보다 이곳이 더 좋았다. 카미악 뷰트에서 내려다본 풍경은 아름답다기보다는 차분하고 넉넉했다. 삶이란 늘 무엇인가를 가꾸고, 계획하고, 또 어느 순간에는 거두는 일의 반복일 텐데, 이 들판은 그 순환이 당연한 듯 품고 있었다.

강한 햇살이 부족하여 사진 찍기는 100%에 미치지 못하였으나 자연의 아름다움과 대지의 풍요로움을 선물로 가득 받은 날이었다.

Was the yellow color seen in Steptoe Butte here? On the side of the road, a cluster of Jerusalem artichoke(wild sunflower) and Coreopsis lanceolata attracted cameras. The yellow color of the two flowers was soft and warm, so it was a color that brightened my heart rather than brightened my eyes. Entering the yellow field, I also became a flower.

When I reached the top, the wind quietly wrapped around my shoulders. There was a gentle breathing between the earth and the sky as if nature were breathing with its whole body. The green wheat field, which stretched to the end of the horizon, gave itself up to the wind. The appearance of the growth and the marks after harvest were seen side by side on one screen.

I liked this place better than the view from Steptoe Butte. The view from Kamiak Butte was calm and ample rather than beautiful. Life will always be a repetition of growing and harvesting something, but this field held the cycle as if it were natural.

The lack of strong sunlight made it less than 100% of the time to take pictures, but it was a day filled with gifts of natural beauty and abundance of the earth.

협곡으로 이어진 펄루스 폭포

5시 알람 소리를 듣고 일출을 담으러 혼자 카미악 뷰트로 갔다. 일출 시각은 5시, 이미 솟은 해를 핸드폰으로 급히 찍고, 길을 나섰다. 이왕 나선 길인데 어제 가지 못한 카미악 뷰트 뒤쪽 산길로 운전했다.

밀밭과 밀밭 사잇길도 지나도, 울퉁불퉁 농로를 거쳐 펄루스(Palouse)라 명명한 마을까지 아침 드라이브를 하였다. 반듯하게 정비된 우리나라 들판과 달리 삐딱한 곳이나 구릉지에도 상관없이 씨를 뿌려 생긴 대로 자연스러운 들판을 보여주었다. 물론 농기구가 한몫하였을 것이다.

숙소로 돌아와서 다시 잠깐 눈을 붙이고 일어났다. 어제 먹다 남은 음식과 삶은 달걀을 추가한 아침을 먹고 도시락까지 만들었다.

이번 여행에서 날씨가 가장 좋은 날이었다. 구름 한 점 없이 깨끗한 하늘은 금방이라도 파란색 물감을 주르르 쏟아낼 것 같았다. 야호, 펄루스 폭포로 출발!

Palouse Fall leading to a canyon

After hearing the 5 a.m. alarm, I went to Kamiak Butte by myself to capture the sunrise. At five o'clock at sunrise, I quickly took a phone shot of the already-risen sun and headed out. Since I was already on the road, I drove along the mountain road behind Kamiak Butte, which I couldn't take yesterday.

I took a morning drive to the village named Palouse after passing the road between the wheat fields and the wheat fields, through the bumpy farm road. Unlike Korea's straight-up fields, it showed natural fields as they were formed by sowing seeds regardless of crooked areas or hilly areas. Of course, farming equipment would have played a part.

When I came back to the accommodation, I slept for a while again and woke up. I ate breakfast with boiled eggs added to the leftovers I ate yesterday and even made a lunch box.

It was the best day on this trip. The clear sky without a cloud seemed like it would pour out blue paint at any moment. Yay, let's go to Palouse Falls!

펄루스 폭포로 향하는 길은 한적하고 고요하였다, 가끔 시원하게 부는 바람 소리와 자동차의 엔진 소리가 고요를 깨뜨렸다. 밀밭을 지나고, 산길을 돌아 길은 굽이굽이 이어졌다.

'음메~~' 울부짖으며 이동하는 소들의 움직임과 그들을 목장에 가두는 일꾼들의 외침이 함께 어우러져 대지를 흔들었다. 다른 초지로 이동하기 위해 소를 모은다고 어릴 때부터 소몰이 일을 하고 있다는 인부가 일러주었다.

무심한 듯 풀을 뜯는 소의 모습은 마치 오래전부터 그곳에 뿌리내린 생명처럼 당당하였다. 소 떼 모습을 찍느라 가까이 다가갔더니 수컷 몇 마리가 공격할 듯이 나를 응시하였다. 그들의 눈빛은 말이 없었으나 침묵 속에 감히 범접할 수 없는 묵직한 존재감을 느꼈다. 수소 나름대로 무리를 지키려는 태도이리라.

소들을 안정시켜 이틀 뒤에 이동할 초지는 6시간 이상 걸린다고 하였다. 사람 7명과 개 두 마리가 그 일을 어떻게 할까 걱정과 궁금증을 뒤로하고 다시 폭포로 향했다.

The road to Palouse Falls was silent and quiet. The sound of the cool wind and the engine of the car sometimes broke the silence. The road winded through wheat fields and around mountain paths.

'Moo~~', the motion of the cattle advancing with loud, echoing bellows, and the cries of the workers trapping the cow on the ranch, combined to shake the earth. A worker told me that he has been working as a cow since he was a child to gather cattle to move to other grasslands.

The sight of the cows grazing nonchalantly was dignified, as if they were life forms that had taken root there long ago. As I approached to take a picture of a herd of cows, some males stared at me like they were attacking me. Their eyes were silent, but they felt a heavy presence that they could not dare to encounter in silence. The bulls must be an attitude to protect the herd in its own way.

It was said that the grasslands to move after two days by stabilizing the cows would take more than 6 hours. Leaving behind the worries and curiosity about how 7 people and 2 dogs would do the job, we headed back to the waterfall.

펄루스 폭포 입구에서 낸 입장료가 주차요금을 대신하였다. 처음 폭포를 보았을 때 풍화와 침식 작용으로 바위가 갈라져 물길이 생기고 협곡이 만들어졌다고 생각하였는데 생성 과정이 달랐다.

아래로 곤두박질치는 물줄기를 바라보았다. 거대한 낙차 앞에서 시간은 거꾸로 흐르는 듯했다. 펄루스 폭포, 그 이름 속에는 태고의 메아리가 숨 쉬고 있었다. 용암 분출도 아니고, 땅이 갈라진 틈도 아니었다. 거대한 빙하기, '미줄라 대홍수(Missoula Floods)'라 불리던 혼돈의 시대에 대지를 집어삼킬 듯이 휩쓸고 간 상흔이자 수만 년의 세월이 깊이 새겨진 지질학적 기록이었다.

협곡은 그랜드캐니언의 축소판 같았다. 웅장함 속에 담긴 정교함, 세월이 빚어낸 층마다 지구가 겪어온 아픔과 성장통이 새겨져 있는 듯했다. 아찔한 깊이로 내려앉은 그 심연 속에서, 빙하가 녹아내린 물이 폭주하듯 대지를 파내고 깎아내려 지금의 독특한 지형을 완성시킨 맹렬함이 느껴졌다. 코로나 전까지 계곡 아래로 내려가 트레킹을 할 수 있었는데 사고가 종종 발생하여 출입이 금지된 상태였다.

The entrance fee at the entrance of Palouse Falls replaced the parking fee. When I first saw the waterfall, I thought that the rocks were divided by weathering and erosion, resulting in waterways and canyons, but the formation process was different.

I looked at the plunging stream of water. Time seemed to have gone backwards in front of the huge drop. Palouse Falls, in its name, was an ancient echo. It wasn't a lava eruption, it wasn't a crack in the ground. In an era of chaos called "Missoula Floods," it was a scar that swept away the earth like it was devoured and a geological record deeply engraved with tens of thousands of years.

The canyon was like a miniature version of the Grand Canyon. The sophistication contained in grandeur and the pain and growth that the earth has suffered in each layer created by the years seemed to be engraved. In the abyss, which fell to a dizzying depth, I felt the ferocity that completed the unique terrain of the present day by digging up and erasing the ground like a torrent of glacial melting water. Before COVID, people were able to go down the valley and trek, but accidents often occurred and people were banned from entering.

강 한쪽에 삼각뿔처럼 뾰족하게 쌓여있던 자갈 더미가 인상적이었다. 단순히 퇴적된 돌멩이 무더기가 아니었다. 폭포 아래로 끊임없이 떨어지고, 부서지고, 쓸려 내려온 시간의 파편들이었다. 수만 년 전의 물이 하나하나의 작은 자갈 알갱이 속에 담겨있는 것이다.

무심히 흘러가는 물길은 내게 앞으로 살아갈 태도를 보여주었다. 유유히 흐르는 부드러움, 암석에 맞서다가도 다시 돌아가는 유연함, 아래로 끝까지 흘러가는 꾸준함과 성실함을. 나이가 들어가면서도 유연하지 못한 나에게 자연은 여러 가르침을 주었다.

펄루스 폭포가 흐르고 흘러 만들어낸 비옥한 곡창지대처럼, 파괴는 결국 새로운 창조의 씨앗이 된다는 자연의 섭리를 목격하였다. 쉼 없이 형체를 바꾸는 물, 그리고 그 물이 빚어낸 또 다른 생명의 터전, 인간의 시간으로는 감히 가늠할 수 없는 대자연의 섭리 앞에서 경외감과 겸손이 밀려왔다. 저 거대한 물줄기 속에서 과거와 현재, 그리고 미래가 하나의 원으로 이어지는 듯한 착각에 빠져들었다.

The pile of pebbles on the side of the river, which was as pointed as a triangular pyramid, was impressive. It wasn't just a pile of deposited stones. They were fragments of time constantly falling, breaking, and being swept down the waterfall. Water from tens of thousands of years ago is contained within each and every tiny grain of gravel.

The carefree flow of water showed me an attitude to live in the future. The softness that flows smoothly, the flexibility that goes back even against the rock, the steadiness and sincerity that flows down to the end. Nature has taught me many things because I am getting older but not flexible.

Like the fertile granary created by the flow of Palouse Falls, destruction eventually became the seed of new creation. In the face of the water that constantly changes shape, another site of life created by it, and the providence of Mother Nature that cannot be measured in human time, awe and humility came. In that huge stream of water, I fell into the illusion that the past, present, and future lead to one circle.

PART
6

우드번

Hallie Ford
Museum of Art
WILLAMETTE
THE FIRST UNIVERSITY IN THE WEST
art

Woodburn

우드번을 향하여

습관처럼 일찍 눈이 떠졌다. 처음 여정에 우드번은 없었다. 린에게 열기구 예약을 부탁하면서 가게 된 곳이다. 열기구를 타려면 새벽 5시까지 집합해야 하는데, 린 집에서는 너무 멀어서 날짜를 바꾸어 우드번에 숙소를 정했다.

펄루스 숙소에는 잔디밭에 물주는 스프링클러가 정해진 시각에 작동하였다. 시골길을 다니느라 거지 신세가 된 차를 스프링클러에서 물이 나오는 각도에 맞추어 세워두고, 자동으로 세차한 덕택에 어느 정도 말끔해졌다. 후배가 운전대를 잡고 일찍 출발하였다. 내가 운전할 때는 바깥 풍경을 볼 여유가 없었는데 운전석 옆에 앉으니 마음에 여유가 생겼다.

3일 동안 밀밭 주변을 다녔으나 밭에서 일하는 사람을 한 명도 보지 못했다. 피를 뽑는 사람도, 농약을 뿌리는 사람도 없었다. 경작지가 워낙 넓어서 기계가 대신하고 있었다. 우드번으로 가는 길에 농기구를 이용해서 작업하는 모습을 발견했다.

농기구를 소재로 한 밀밭을 찍고 싶었다. 차량이 많지 않아 차를 세워달라고 부탁했는데 후배는 지레 겁을 먹고 계속 달렸다. 순간의 포착, 찰나의 예술이 멀리 달아나 버렸다. 머물렀던 우드번 호텔방에 농기구를 소재로 찍은 사진을 보니 아쉬운 마음이 더 컸다. 도시에 접어들자 후배를 대신해서 내가 운전석에 앉았다.

Towards Woodburn

My woke up early as a habit. There was no Woodburn on the first journey. I went there when I asked Lynn to make a reservation for a hot air balloon. We had to gather by 5 a.m. to ride the hot air balloon, but it was too far from Lynn's house, so we changed the date and stayed in Woodburn.

In the Palouse accommodation, sprinklers watering the lawn operated at a fixed time. The car, which had become a beggar while traveling on the country road, was parked at the angle at which the water came out of the sprinkler, and it was cleaned to some extent thanks to the automatic car wash. My junior took the wheel and left early. I couldn't afford to look outside when I was driving, but sitting next to the driver's seat made me feel relaxed.

I went around the wheat field for three days, but I didn't see any of them working in the field. There was no one pulling weeds or spraying pesticides. The arable land was so large that machines were taking over. On the way to Woodburn, I found people working with farm equipment.

I wanted to film a wheat field based on agricultural equipment. There were not many vehicles, so I asked my junior to pull over, but she was scared and kept running. The capture of the moment, the art of the moment, went far away. I was more disappointed to see the picture of the farm equipment in the Woodburn Hotel room where I stayed. When we entered the city, I drove on behalf of my junior.

할리 포드 미술관에서

예정 시각보다 일찍 도착하여 우드번에서 가까운 세일럼(Salem)으로 갔다. 시청사에서 걸어서 갈 수 있는 곳이 대학, 미술관, 공원 등이었다. 먼저 들른 1998년에 개관한 미술관은 윌라멧 대학 소속이었다. 원주민 예술과 고대 문명 유물을 보유하여 학생들의 교육 자료로 활용한다고 하였다. 오리건주 출신 예술가들의 기획전을 관람하였다. 작은 도시인데도 대학이 지역의 중심이 되어 주민과 예술가를 위해 후원하고 있다는 사실이 부러웠다.

고대와 현대의 만남, 자연으로부터 얻은 것과 인위적인 작품을 보았다. 척박한 환경에서 살기 위해 고군분투한 원주민들의 삶이 보였다. 실생활에 썼던 여러 가지 도구와 옷, 그리고 그들이 만든 생활용품도 창작품이 되었다. 아시안과 비슷한 그들의 모습과 생활상에 친근감이 느껴졌다. 반면, 사회를 풍자한 현대 그림은 화학 냄새를 잔뜩 품은 안료 성분만큼 이해하기 어려웠다. 작품마다 가진 가치를 다 알 수는 없었지만 내 기억 속의 일부가 되었다.

At the Hallie Ford Museum of Art

I arrived earlier than scheduled and went to Salem, close to Woodburn. Universities, art galleries, and parks were within walking distance of the city hall. The museum, which first opened in 1998, belonged to Willamet University. It is said that indigenous art and ancient civilization artifacts are retained and used as educational materials for students. I watched a special exhibition by artists from Oregon. Even though it was a small city, I envied the fact that the university became the center of the region and sponsored it for residents and artists.

I saw the encounter between ancient and modern times, what natural had given and what humans had created. The lives of indigenous people who struggled to live in barren conditions were visible. Various tools and clothes used in real life, and household items they made became creative works. I felt familiarity with their appearance and life similar to those of Asian countries. On the other hand, the modern painting that satirized society was as difficult to understand as the pigment composition that contained a chemical odor. I couldn't know all the value of each piece, but it became part of my memory.

그녀의 리즈 시절은?

직원들의 친절을 뒤로하고 밖으로 나왔다. 시청사 옆 공원에서 아침에 준비한 샌드위치를 먹었다. 점심시간이라 공원 벤치에서 점심을 먹는 사람도 있었다. 여행하는 동안, 시간도 경비도 절약할 겸 종종 점심을 이런 식으로 먹었다.

공원에 있는 사람들을 바라보고 있었을 때, 반 노출 옷차림으로 속옷을 아무렇게나 내보이는 행동을 하는 사람이 눈에 들어왔다. 온전한 정신은 아닌 듯했다. 아니나 다를까, 그녀가 쓰레기통을 뒤적이며 버려진 음식을 찾는 모습에서 인간의 존엄성이 아닌, 생존의 본능이 느껴졌다.

삶은 계란 하나와 삶은 감자 몇 개를 그녀에게 주었다. 그녀는 의심의 눈초리도 없이 조심스럽게 그것을 받았다. 미소 띤 그녀의 얼굴에서, 오래전 잊고 지냈던 그녀의 인간적인 접촉에 대한 그리움을 읽을 수 있었다.

자신에게 관심을 보여준 나에게 뭔가 보답이라도 하려는 듯 자기의 핸드백을 뒤적였다. 오래된 성경책에서 꺼낸 성물처럼 성모마리아 엽서 한 장을 나에게 주었다. 오래되었지만 그녀에게는 소중한 무언가였으리라. 묵주를 끼고 있지 않았으나 그녀는 가톨릭 신자였던 것일까.

When was her prime years?

I left the staff's kindness behind and went outside. I ate a sandwich that I prepared in the morning at the park next to the city hall. Some people had lunch on the park bench because it was lunchtime. During the trip, I often had lunch like this to save time and money.

As I was looking at the people in the park, I noticed someone who was dressed in semi-exposed clothes and showed off their underwear at random. She didn't seem to be of sound mind. Sure enough, the instinct for survival, not human dignity, was felt in her search for discarded food through trash cans.

I handed her a boiled egg and some boiled potatoes. She received it carefully, without a doubt. On her smiley face, I could read the longing for her human touch, which she had forgotten a long time ago.

She rummaged through her handbag as if to repay me for showing interest in her. She gave me a post card of the Virgin Mary, like a holy object taken out of an old Bible. It was an old, but it must have been something precious to her. Was she a Catholic even though she wasn't wearing a rosary?

나보다 작은 키를 가진 그녀는 금발에 동그란 얼굴로 귀여운 모습이 남아있었다. 유달리 붉은 얼굴과 코 주변이 붉은 것으로 보아 이미 알코올 중독자가 된 듯했다. 그녀에게도 분명 꽃다운 시절이 있었을 테지. 신 앞에 무릎 꿇고 기도하는 소녀 시절, 누군가와 사람에 빠진 적도, 희망과 꿈을 실현해서 행복한 시절도 있었을 터. 어쩌다 저렇게 그녀의 삶이 부서진 것일까.

우리는 살면서 정상과 비정상을 나누고, 도움을 주는 쪽과 받는 쪽 사이에 경계를 긋는다. 공원에서 마주한 그녀와 나는 그런 구분이 아니었다. 사람과 사람 사이의 눈 맞춤, 마음의 교환이었다.

그녀는 나와의 만남으로 잊고 살았던 그녀의 리즈 시절을 잠깐이라도 떠올렸을까. 그녀를 향했던 나의 관심이 그녀에게 힘이 되었으면 좋겠다. 부서진 그녀의 삶이 돌아올 수는 없겠지만, 그녀 자신이 얼마나 소중한 존재임을 잊지 말기를 기도하였다.

Shorter than me, she remained cute with blonde hair and a round face. Her nose and exceptionally red face, she already seemed to be an alcoholic. I'm sure, she must have had her prime of youth. There must have been times when she was a girl kneeling in front of God and praying, when she fell in love with someone, and when she realized her hopes and dreams, she must have been happy. How did her life break like that?

When we live, we divide normal and abnormal, and draw a boundary between the helping and the receiving. She and I, who faced each other in the park, were not that distinction. It was eye contact and exchange of mind between people.

Did she even briefly recall her Leeds days, which she had forgotten because of the meeting with me? I hope my interest in her will help her. Her broken life will never come back, but I prayed that she would not forget how precious she was.

공원 근처에 있는 윌라멧(Willamette) 대학으로 갔다. 1842년에 세워진 대학은 미국 서부에서 가장 오래된 사립대학이다. 담장도, 수위도 없고, 주말이라 학생들도 없어서 여유롭게 사진 찍기에 좋았다. 잘 가꿔진 정원과 벤치 등 공원과 다름없었다.

졸업을 앞둔 청년 둘이 사진을 찍고 있었다. 한국은 대학 졸업 가운이 모두 검은색인데 이곳은 빨간색이었다. 개인의 자유를 존중하는 미국답게 이 대학의 상징 같았다. 대학 건물처럼 빨간 가운이 그들에게 좋은 기운이 되어 원하는 바가 이루어지면 좋겠다.

I went to Willamette University near the park. Founded in 1842, the university is the oldest private university in the western United States. There was no fence, no janitor and there were no students on the weekend, so it was good to take pictures leisurely. It was like a park, with well-groomed gardens and benches.

Two young men who were about to graduate were taking pictures. In Korea, college graduation gowns are all black, but this place was red. It was like a symbol of this university as an USA who respects individual freedom. I hope that red gowns like university buildings will be a good energy for them and what they want will be achieved.

처음 보는 성인식

잔디밭에 놓인 벤치에 앉아 긴장감과 피곤함을 달래며 쉬었다. 대학에서 보이는 주의사당은 학생들에게 어떤 자극제가 될까. 내가 쉬고 있는 벤치와 잔디밭 역시 공부하다 지친 학생들의 좋은 휴식처가 될 것이다.

떠들썩한 소리를 따라 걸으니 사진사를 대동한 한 무리의 소녀와 소년들이 주인공이었다. 한 여학생이 16세가 되어 성인식 이벤트 중이라고 누군가가 말해주었다. 나라마다, 정부 부처마다 성인의 나이 기준이 다름을 알고 있었으나 미국에서는 16세가 성인이라니 놀라웠다.

학업도 채 끝나지 않은 어린 학생에게 성인의 의미란 무엇일까? 성인의 자격은 복잡한 증명서나 값비싼 의상에서 나오지 않는다. 자신의 말에 책임지려는 행동, 타인의 목소리에 귀 기울이는 습관, 작은 날들 속에서 반복되는 잘못을 바로잡으려는 태도에서 자랄 것이다. 성인 의식은 시작을 알리는 종소리일 뿐, 진짜 성숙은 종소리가 울린 뒤, 길 위에서 발에 차이는 모래처럼 시간이 쌓여 만들어진다.

Witnessing a Coming-of-age ceremony for the first time

Sitting on a bench on the lawn, I rested, soothing my tension and tiredness. What kind of stimulus will the state capitol near the university be for students? The bench and lawn where I am resting will also be a good resting place for students who are tired of studying.

Walking along with the loud sound, a group of girls and boys accompanied by photographers were the main characters. Someone told me that a female student was in the midst of a coming-of-age ceremony after turning 16. I knew that the age of adulthood varied from country to country and government to government, but I was surprised to learn tht in the the United States, 16 is considered adulthood.

What is the meaning of adulthood for a young student who has not even completed her studies? Adult qualifications do not come from complicated certificates or expensive dress. She will grow from the behavior of taking responsibility for her words, the habit of listening to the voices of others, and the attitude of correcting repeated mistakes in small days. Adult rituals are just the bells that announce the beginning, and real maturity is created by accumulating time like sand on the road after the bells ring.

결혼식 들러리들은 종종 보았는데 성인식 들러리들은 처음 보았다. 들러리로 선 다섯 남학생과 다섯 여학생은 마치 합주단의 악보처럼 배치되어 있었다. 주인공의 드레스가 바람에 부드럽게 출렁거렸고, 햇살은 작은 진주처럼 반짝이다가 이내 소녀의 어깨 위로 조용히 내려앉았다. 들러리들의 장난기 섞인 표정에 주인공 입가에 미소가 번졌다. 사진사의 셔터 소리에 그들의 장난과 웃음은 잠시 멈추었다 다시 흘렀다.

돈은 의식을 치르는 데 필요하나 성인의 자격을 사 오지는 못한다. 옷 대여비와 촬영비, 함께한 식사비 계산서는 곧 사라질 숫자들이다. 그 숫자들은 부모의 몫이다. 부자 부모를 가진 주인공을 부러워하며 우리도 그들 속 일원이 되어 사진으로 남겼다.

I've often seen wedding bridesmaids but first seen coming-of-age and bridesmaids. The five boys and five girls who stood as bridesmaids were arranged like sheet music of an ensemble. The protagonist's dress gently swayed in the wind, and the sunlight sparkled like small pearls before setting quietly on the girl's shoulders. The playful expressions of the bridesmaids brought a smile to heroine. Their mischief and laughter paused at the photographer's shutter and flowed again.

Money is necessary for ceremonies, but it does not buy adult qualifications. The cost of renting clothes, filming, and meals together are numbers that will soon disappear. The numbers are down to the parents. Envious of the main character who has rich parents, we became part of them and took pictures.

비싼 우드번 아울렛

숙소가 있는 우드번까지 약 20분이 걸렸다. 숙소 입구를 놓치고 지나쳤더니 우드번 아울렛 매장 입구가 나왔다.

필요한 운동복을 사려고 한 매장에 들어갔다. 미국서 생산되는 것이라 저렴할 줄 알았는데 한국에서 사는 것과 같은 가격이라서 사지 않았다. 딸이 부탁한 가방을 사기 위해 관련 매장으로 향했다. 마찬가지로 인터넷에서 파는 가격과 같았고, 인터넷에서 보았던 제품 중에 없는 것이 많았다. 아울렛 매장이라는 뜻이 무색할 정도로 실망감이 컸다.

현지인들은 미국 물가가 워낙 비싸기 때문인지, 정상가보다 많이 싸다고 생각하는지 고민 없이 척척 골라 담는 행동에 깜짝 놀랐다. 한 아주머니는 바지, 윗도리, 원피스 등 다섯 가지나 사서 나는 놀란 토끼가 되었다.

내가 머물렀던 호스트들은 대부분 좋은 직업에서 퇴직한 중산층이었다. 낡은 백을 들고 다니고, 오래된 살림살이를 버리지 않고 쓰며, 수수한 차림새의 평범한 옆집 아저씨 아주머니 같은 분들이었다. 나 역시 유행을 가리지 않고 오래된 옷을 입고, 에코백을 들고 다니며, 외모에 크게 신을 쓰지 않는다. 명품을 살 돈이면 여행을 한 번 더 간다는 생각으로 살아왔다. 비싼데 여기까지 와서 왜 사? 안 사도 괜찮아, 스스로 위안하며 아울렛 매장을 빠져나왔다.

Expensive Woodburn Outlet

It took about 20 minutes to get to the Woodburn accommodation. I missed the entrance to the hotel and passed by, and I came out of the entrance to the Woodburn outlet store.

I entered a store to buy the sportswear I needed. I thought it would be cheap because it was produced in the United States, but I didn't buy it because it was the same price as buying it in Korea. I headed to the related store to buy the bag my daughter asked for. Similarly, it was the same as the price sold on the Internet, and there were many products that were not seen on the Internet. I was so disappointed that the meaning of an outlet store was meaningless.

I was surprised by the act of picking without worrying about whether the price of the U.S. was so high or if the locals thought it was cheaper than the normal price. One lady bought five items, including pants, tops, and dresses, so I was shocked.

Most of the hosts I stayed at were middle-class, retired from good jobs. They carried old bags, used old housekeeping without throwing it away, and were ordinary next door men and ladies in modest clothes. I, too, wear old clothes without being fashionable, carry an eco bag instead of a famous luxury bag, and don't really wear much on my appearance. I have lived with the idea of going on another trip if I have money to buy luxury goods. It's expensive, why do I come here and buy it? It's okay not to buy it, I left the outlet store comforting myself.

취소된 열기구

알람 소리를 듣고 눈 뜬 시각은 새벽 4시였다. 오로라(AURORA) 비행장까지 먼 거리는 아니었으나 도착하니 4시 50분이었다. 유명 관광지가 아니라서 일행은 우리 둘과 부부 한 팀뿐이었다. 아무리 둘러보아도 관계자는 보이지 않았다. 사무실 문이 닫혀서 연락처를 찾기 위해 핸드폰을 뒤적였다. 얼마나 급했으면 새벽에 취소 메일을 보냈을까. 차라리 전화를 해주지.

바람이 심해서 안전상의 이유로 열기구를 띄울 수 없다는 내용이었다. 땅에서는 바람이 잔잔한데, 고도가 높아질수록 바람이 세어진다는 말인가. 한 치 앞도 알 수 없는 자연의 변화다. 우리의 삶도 이와 다르지 않다. 맑다가도 바람이 불고, 비가 내리듯이, 우리 삶에도 힘든 일도 생기고, 뜻밖의 고난이 찾아들기도 한다. 인생이 마음먹은 대로 술술 풀린다면 얼마나 좋을까.

Cancelled hot air balloon

It was 4 a.m. when I woke up after hearing the alarm. It wasn't a long distance to Aurora Airport, when I arrived at 4:50. It wasn't a famous tourist destination, so there was only two of us and a couple. No matter how much I looked around, I couldn't see anyone involved. The office door was closed, so I rummaged through my phone to find them. How urgent it must have been to send a cancellation email early in the morning? They should have called me instead.

It was said that the hot air balloon could not be floated for safety reasons because of the strong wind. The wind was calm on the ground, I couldn't believe that the higher the altitude, the stronger the wind. It is a change in nature that cannot be known an inch ahead. Our lives are like changes in the weather. Just as it is clear, the wind blows, and the rain falls, there are difficulties in our lives, and unexpected hardships come. I wish my life would be solved as I decided.

날씨를 무시하고 4명을 태워 열기구를 띄웠다면 아마도 벌금이 더 많았을 것이다. 안전을 우선으로 둔 결정이라서 할 말이 없었으나 나로서는 정말 속상한 일이었다. 열기구를 타기 위해 일정을 바꿔서 우드번에서 자고, 새벽같이 일어났는데…. 하늘에서 내려다보는 윌라멧 밸리, 후버 산과, 마운트 아담스 등의 조망은 상상 속에 남겨야 했다.

나온 김에 일출이나 찍자고 적당한 장소를 찾으러 이리저리 다녔다. 부산이나 제주처럼 높은 곳도 없고, 바다는 더더욱 없어서 원하던 일출은 찍지 못했다. 도시에서 벗어난 외곽이라서 농촌 냄새가 물씬 풍겼다. 아침 햇살이 연둣빛 묘목 잎 사이로 스며들어 잎맥을 은은하게 밝혀주었다. 묘목은 마치 하루를 새롭게 시작하는 듯 잎사귀에 맺힌 이슬방울을 오랫동안 품었다.

If they ignored the weather and picked up four people to float the hot air balloon, maybe the fine would have been higher. I had nothing to say because it was a safety-first decision, but it was really upsetting for me. I changed my schedule to get on the hot air balloon, slept in Woodburn, woke up early in the morning…. The view of the Willamet Valley, the Hoover Mountains, and Mount Adams from the sky had to be left in the imagination.

Since I came out, I went around looking for a suitable place to take a picture of the sunrise. There was no high place like Busan or Jeju, and there was no sea, so I couldn't take the sunrise I wanted. It was outside of the city, so it had a strong rural feel. The morning sun permeated through the leaves of the green seedlings and gently illuminated the veins of the leaves. The seedlings had long embraced the dewdrops on their leaves, as if they were starting their day anew.

가라지 세일

우드번에서 다시 시애틀로 가야 했다. 시애틀에 렌터카를 반납하고 이틀 뒤, 밴쿠버로 가야 했기 때문이었다. 아침에 열기구를 못 타서 시간이 남았다. 고속도로 이용이 가장 빠른 길이었지만 마을 구경을 할 요량으로 국도를 이용하였다.

얼마 가지 않아서 가라지(garage) 세일 하는 장소에 들렀다. 해외여행에서 이런 곳이나 토요 마켓 등에 종종 들르곤 했다. 우리와 다른 그들의 오래전 문화를 알 수 있을 뿐만 아니라 구경하는 것이 흥미로웠기 때문이었다. 마을 회원들이 고정적으로 창고에 물건을 보관해 두었다가 주말에 판다고 하였다.

의식주에 관련된 물건이 엄청 많았다. 가라지 세일을 둘러보던 그 순간, 마음 한구석이 묘하게 찌르르해졌다. 작은 나사부터 오래된 출입문 문짝까지, 지나치는 물건 하나하나가 그들의 지난 세월을 어렴풋이 보여주는 듯했다. 잡동사니에 불과했지만, 그 속엔 누군가의 삶의 조각들이 고스란히 담겨있었다.

Garage Sale

I had to go back to Seattle from Woodburn. Because I must return my rental car to Seattle and go to Vancouver two days later. I had some time left because I couldn't ride the hot air balloon in the morning. The highway was the fastest way, but we used the general road to see the village.

After a while, I stopped by a place with a garage sale. I often stopped by these places or Saturday markets on overseas trips. It was interesting not only to learn about their ancient culture, which was different from ours, but also to observe it. The village members said they kept things in the warehouse regularly and then sold them on weekends.

There were a lot of things related to food, clothing, and shelter. The moment I was looking around the Garage sale, a corner of my heart felt strangely prickled. From small screws to old entrance doors, every passing object seemed to obscure their past years. It was just a clutter, but there were pieces of someone's life intact.

몇 세대 전에 사용했을 촛대는 은은한 광택 속에 고풍스러운 기품을 품고 있었다. 금박이 벗겨진 접시는 한때 누군가의 소중한 저녁 식탁을 장식했을 것을 생각하니 괜스레 가슴이 뭉클해졌다. 낡고 헤진 장난감들에서는 아이들의 웃음소리가 들려올 것만 같았고, 낡은 서류 가방 하나에도 바쁘게 살았을 누군가의 청춘이 오롯이 녹아있었다. 누가 사갈까 싶은 녹슨 조리용 도구도 자리를 잡고 있었다.

그저 낡고 쓸모없는 물건들이라고 생각했지만, 애틋함과 아련함, 아주 약간의 외로움 등 복잡한 마음이 들었다. 사람들은 떠났으나 물건들은 여전히 주인을 기다리고 있지 않은지. 내가 무심코 지나쳐 버렸을 시간이 이곳에서는 여전히 숨 쉬고 있는 듯해서 발걸음을 쉽게 떼지 못했다.

The candlestick, which would have been used a few generations ago, had an antique style in its subtle gloss. The plate with the gold leaf peeled off moved my heart to think that the plate once decorated someone's precious dinner table. The old and worn toys seemed to hear children's laughter. The youth of someone who would have been busy living in an old briefcase was melted. There were also rusty cooking utensils on display, wondering who would buy them.

I thought they were just old and useless things, but I had mixed feelings, such as warmth, sadness, a little bit of loneliness, People have left but things are still waiting for their owners. The time that I would have inadvertently passed seemed to be still breathing here, so I couldn't take my step easily.

내비게이션이 안내하는 곳으로 운전하면서 지나쳤던 어느 곳은 도로와 마을이 너무 예뻐서 무작정 차를 세웠다. 예쁜 꽃을 보니 제각각 정원을 가꾼 이들과 마을 길을 가꾼 사람들의 고운 마음이 느껴졌다.

집들은 대부분 2층이었다. 앞뜰에 핀 철쭉류, 캘리포니아 양귀비, 니포피아 등 활짝 핀 꽃들이 우리를 환영해 주었다. 훤히 보이는 담장 안으로 작은 정자를 지어 휴식 공간을 마련한 집도 있었다. 난쟁이 조각 시리즈가 있는 뜰, 비너스 같은 아름다운 조각품 등이 행인을 미소 짓게 만들었다. 창문 옆 귀퉁이에 성조기를 걸어둔 집주인은 틀림없는 애국자이리라. 집 안은 또 얼마나 예쁘게 꾸며놓았을까 궁금하게 여기며 다양한 집들을 한참 구경하였다.

While driving to a place guided by the navigation system, I passe by a place where the road and village were so beautiful that I stopped the car without thinking. Looking at the pretty flowers, I felt the beautiful hearts of people who cared for the garden from house to house and those who maintained the village roads.

Most of the houses were two-story houses. In the front yard, flowers in full bloom welcomed us, such as royal azaleas, California poppies, and nipofia. There was also a house where a small pavilion was built inside a clear wall to provide a resting place. The courtyard with its series of dwarf sculptures and beautiful sculptures like Venus brought smiles to passersby. The landlord who hung the American flag on the corner next to the window must be a patriot. I looked around various houses for a long time wondering how beautiful inside of the house was decorated.

다시 시애틀로

Back to Seattle

스타벅스 리저브 로스터리

스타벅스 1호점이 너무 비좁고 협소하여 2014년에 자동차 전시장 건물을 매입하여 재탄생 시킨 커피 예술 공간이었다. 가게 안으로 들어서는 순간 고소한 커피 향이 온몸을 감쌌다. 눈앞에 펼쳐진 공간은 단순한 카페가 아니라 커피의 세계로 초대하는 극장 같았다.

구릿빛 로스팅 기계들이 설치된 공간은 깨끗한 커피 공장이었다. 볶음 콩처럼 느껴지는 갓 볶은 원두를 사고 싶었으나 커피를 마시면 잠을 이루지 못해서 보는 것으로 만족하였다. 커피를 마시려는 고객이 메인 바에서 길게 줄을 서서 기다렸다. 바리스타들의 손끝에서 정교한 라떼 아트가 꽃처럼 피어났다. 커피 관련 장비, 여러 종류의 기념품을 팔았다. 커피 이야기를 들으며 체험하는 프로그램도 있다고 들었으나 시간이 충분하지 않아 발길을 돌렸다.

Starbucks Reserve Roastery

The first Starbucks store was so cramped and narrow that it was a coffee art space that was reborn by purchasing an automobile exhibition hall building in 2014. As soon as I entered the store, the savory coffee scent enveloped my whole body. The space in front of my eyes was not just a cafe, but a theater inviting me to the world of coffee.

The space where the copper roasting machines were installed was a clean coffee factory. I wanted to buy freshly fried beans that felt like stir-fried beans, but when I drank coffee, I couldn't sleep, so I was satisfied with seeing them. A customer waiting in a long line for coffee at the main bar. Elaborate latte art blossomed like flowers at the baristas' fingertips. They sold coffee-related equipment and various kinds of souvenirs. I heard that there is a program where we can experience it while listening to coffee stories, but I turned away because I didn't have enough time.

ARRIVIAMO

RRIVIAMO
BAR
VIEW MENU

SUMMER IS
FOR TRAVEL

바바라 댁에서

작은 길에서 빠져나와 고속도로로 달렸다. 오늘 우리가 머물 호스트 바바라(Barbara) 가족에게 대접할 음식 재료를 사기 위해 H 마트에 들렀다. 완성된 한국 음식을 파는 편의점이라 우리가 살 음식 재료는 없었다. 검색해서 아시안 마트로 찾아가니 생각보다 다양한 제품을 갖추고 있어서 원하던 재료를 고를 수 있었다.

바바라 남편, 브락(Brock)이 워싱턴 대학에서 IT 과목을 가르치고 있어서 대학에서 가까운 곳에 집이 있었다. 주소대로 찾아가니 집 앞에 한글로 "환영"이라고 써 붙인 문구가 감동이었다. 작은 행동 하나가 얼마나 사람을 행복하게 만드는지!

브락이 썼다는데, 한국 미군 부대에서 통역을 했던 친구 덕분에 한국어도 조금씩 공부하는 중이라고 하였다. 몇 년 뒤 한국을 방문하게 되면 한국어로 의사소통이 가능하겠지. 일요일이라 그녀의 가족 모두 집에 머물면서 우리를 기다리고 있었다.

앞에서 보면 이층집, 안으로 들어가면 3층짜리 집이었다. 반지하에 우리가 머문 방과 화장실, 세탁실과 브락의 사무실이 있고, 1층에는 거실과 식당이 있고, 2층에는 부부방과 딸 방, 게스트 룸과 화장실이 있었다.

At Barbara's house

I got out of the little road and ran on the highway. I stopped by H Mart to buy food ingredients to serve to my host Barbara's family, whom we will be staying with today. There was no food ingredient for us to buy because it was a convenience store selling cooked Korean food. When I searched and went to Asian Mart, I was able to choose the ingredients I wanted because there were more diverse products than I thought.

Barbara's husband, Brock, is a professor of IT at University of Washington, so they had a house close to the university. When I went to the address, I was deeply moved by the phrase "welcome" written in Korean in front of the house. How much happiness a small action can make!

Brock said that he was studying Korean little by little thanks to a friend who interpreted in the U.S. military in Korea. When he visited Korea a few years later, he seemed to be able to communicate in Korean. It was Sunday, so all her family was staying at home waiting for us.

From the front, it was a two-story house, and from the inside, it was a three-story house. There was a room, a bathroom, a laundry room and Brock's office on the semi-basement floor, a living room and a kitchen on the first floor, and a main room, a daughter's room, a guest room and a bathroom on the second floor.

브락이 저녁을 준비할 동안 딸, 엘레아노(Eleanor)가 집 구경을 시켜주었다. 앞뜰에는 아기자기한 꽃밭에 큰 나무가 수호신처럼 서 있는데 그 위에 작은 오두막이 있었다. 동화책에서나 볼 수 있는 것으로 어린 딸을 위해 아빠가 만들어준 것이었다. 이제 자기가 많이 자라서 들어가기 힘들다며 어린 시절의 추억에 잠겼다.

뒤뜰에는 잘 만들어진 닭장이 있었다. 네 마리 닭이 있었는데 라쿤이 물고 가고 두 마리만 남았다고 하였다. 닭은 깃털이 엄청 부드럽고 온순한 종이었다. 튼튼하게 닭장을 다시 짓고, 위쪽에는 그물을 친 상태였다. 상추, 오이 등 채소를 가꾸는데 새들이 쪼아 먹어서 잎들이 망가졌고, 한쪽에는 특별히 그물망을 덮어 키우는 딸기가 빨갛게 익어가고 있었다.

저녁 시간까지 한참 기다려야 해서 선물을 먼저 드렸다. 한복 모양 와인 커버, 두 쌍의 수저 세트, 누비로 만들어진 파우치, 제주도가 그려진 스카프, 그리고 태극부채 등, 다른 집에도 똑같이 드린 선물이었다. 우리가 선물을 너무 많이 가져왔다며 놀라워했다. 엘레아노에게 특별히 무릎 담요를 주었더니 웃음 많은 그녀는 "오 마이 갓(O my God!)"을 연발하며 소리를 지르고, 허리에 두르는 등 소녀다운 행동으로 즐거워하였다.

While Brock was preparing dinner, his daughter Eleanor showed us around the house. In the front garden, a large tree stood like a guardian in a cute flower garden, and there was a small hut on top of it. It was something that her father made for her young daughter, which can only be seen in fairy tales. She seemed to go back to her childhood, saying it was hard to get in after growing up a lot, now.

There was a well-made henhouse in the backyard. Originally, there were four chickens, but a raccoon took them and said that only two were left. Chickens were extremely soft and gentle in their feathers. The henhouse was firmly rebuilt and a net was placed on the top. While cultivating vegetables such as lettuce, and cucumbers, the leaves were damaged because birds pecked at them, and strawberries, which were specifically raised by covering a mesh, were ripening red on one side.

I had to wait a long time until dinner time, so I gave them presents first. It was a gift given to other houses as well, such as a hanbok-shaped wine cover, two pairs of cutlery sets, a quilted pouch, a scarf with Jeju Island on it, and a Taegeuk fan. They were surprised that we brought too many gifts. I gave Eleanor a knee blanket in particular, she was amused by her girlish behavior, shouting and laughing, and putting a blanket around her waist, continuously, "Oh my God!"

브락이 오븐에 구운 닭고기와 샐러드를 저녁으로 세팅해 두고, 그는 오래전에 정해진 저녁 약속을 위해 외출하였다. 우리는 바바라, 딸과 같이 식사하면서 여러 가지 이야기를 나누었다. 가족 모두 올여름에 일본을 여행하는데 한국은 가지 않는다고 해서 섭섭하였다. 그동안 휴스턴에 사는 친구가 자기 집에 머물며 닭이랑 식물을 돌본다고 하였다. 사람을 믿고 사랑하며, 환경을 지키는 찐 서바스 정신을 실천하는 가족이었다.

브락은 식사를 마치고 빨리 돌아왔다. 일상인 것처럼 그는 딸과 함께 야간 산책하는데 우리도 함께 걸었다. 그린레이크는 5만 년 전 빙하에 의해 생겼는데 1910년부터 시에서 공원으로 조성하기 시작하였다.

2.8마일(약 4.5km)의 둘레길을 따라 걷는데 카약, 페달보트 등이 보여 낮에는 수상활동을 할 수 있는 곳 같았다. 여름에는 수영과 허락된 곳에서 낚시도 가능하다고 하였다. 곳곳에 농구 축구, 야구, 수영 등 운동을 할 수 있는 시설과 어린이 놀이터 등 다양한 시설이 잘 갖추어져 있었다. 자연환경도 즐기고, 주변에 상가도 있어서 가족의 피크닉 장소로도 적당하겠다.

어둠이 내려앉은 호수는 잿빛 하늘을 품고 있었고, 물가에는 온종일 자맥질하던 오리들이 쏟아지는 잠에 고개를 끄덕이고 있었다. 개와 함께 산책하는 이의 발걸음은 부드러운 리듬을 남기고, 조깅하는 사람의 숨소리는 고요 속에 작은 생동감을 더했다. 누군가 타는 자전거 바퀴는 지나간 하루의 흔적을 따라 굴러갔다.

Brock setting up oven-baked chicken and salad for dinner, he went out for a long-established dinner appointment. We talked about various things while eating with Barbra and Eleanor. Her family is going to Japan this summer, but I was disappointed that they did not go to Korea. In the meantime, a friend's family living in Houston said they would stay at her house and take care of chickens and plants. It was a family that believed in people, loved them, and practiced the spirit of the true Servas that protected the environment.

Brock came back quickly after finishing his meal. As usual, he took a night walk with his daughter, and we walked together. Green Lake was created by glaciers 50,000 years ago, and the city began making it a park since 1910.

As I walked along the 2.8mile(about 4.5km), I saw kayaks and pedal boats, I thought do water activities during the day. In summer, swimming and fishing where allowed are also possible. There were various facilities such as basketball, soccer, baseball, swimming, etc. and children's playgrounds. It would be suitable as a picnic place for families because they can enjoy the natural environment and there is a shopping mall nearby.

The lake, where darkness had fallen, harbored a gray sky, nodding to the slumber of ducks who had been dipping all day at the water. The footsteps of the walker with the dog left a gentle rhythm, and the jogger's breath added a little liveliness to the stillness. The wheels of someone's bike rolled along the trail of the past day.

워싱턴 대학 방문

브락이 워싱턴 대학을 안내해 준다더니 잊은 듯해서 우리끼리 갔다. 대학 입구 주변 양쪽 길에 아치를 만들며 늘어선 가로수는 제주의 숲길처럼 이어졌다. 나무가 내뿜는 신선한 공기 덕분에 기분이 좋아졌다.

박물관 앞에 주차했는데 한 노신사가 주차비를 결제하기에 이곳도 선결제하는지 여쭈었다. 대학에서 한국 분을 만나니 더 반가웠다. 메모리얼 데이(Memorial Day)라서 모르겠다며, 자기를 따라오라고 하더니 무료 주차 장소로 인도하였다.

서울대서 20년간 정치학을 가르치다가 이곳에 와서 교수를 하는데 정년이 없다고 하셨다. 한국이 싫지 않았으나 직장 때문에 이주하신 듯했다. 요즘 정치판을 보고 있으면 나도 한국을 떠나고 싶다. 우리가 길을 모를까 봐 도서관까지 데려다주고 당신의 연구실로 가셨다. 짧은 만남이었지만 참 멋진 신사분으로 기억에 남았다.

「해리 포터」 영화로 유명해진 도서관이라고 해서 들어가고 싶은데 문이 닫혀있었다. 다행히 1시에 문을 연다고 하였다. 오후에 다시 찾아온 것을 환영이라도 하듯 아침에 흐렸던 하늘이 파란색으로 웃고 있었다. 뾰족한 첨탑이 짧아진 신고딕 양식이 조각된 도서관 외관은 하나의 성처럼 웅장하였다.

Visiting University of Washington

Brock said he was going to show us around the University of Washington, but he seemed to forget, so we went on our own. The street trees lined up with arches on both sides of the road around the entrance to the university continued like a forest road in Jeju. The fresh air from the trees made me feel better.

I parked in front of the museum, and an old gentleman paid for the parking fee, so I asked if this place would also pay in advance. It was more nice to meet a Korean at university. He said he didn't know because it was Memorial Day, and he told us to follow him and led us to a free parking spot.

He taught political science at Seoul National University for 20 years and came here to teach, but he said there was no retirement age. It seemed like he didn't hate Korea, but moved there because of work. Watching the political scene these days, I feel like leaving Korea, too. In case we didn't know the way, he took us to the library and went to his lab. It was a short meeting, but it was memorable as a wonderful gentleman.

I wanted to enter the library because it became famous for Harry Potter movies, but the door was closed. Fortunately, it would open at 1 o'clock. As if to welcome back in the afternoon, the cloudy sky in the morning was smiling blue. The exterior of the library, carved in neo-Gothic style with shorter pointed spires, looked magnificent like a castle.

수잘로 & 알렌 도서관에 들어서는 순간, 마치 호그와트에 발을 들인 듯한 착각이 들었다. 많은 사람이 착각하고 있으나 이곳에서 「해리 포터」 영화를 찍은 적이 없었고, 도서관 내부가 비슷하여 호그와트를 연상시키기에 충분하였다. 천장을 향해 솟은 고딕 양식의 아치들은 웅장하여 경외심마저 들었다. 유리창으로 들어오는 햇살은 책장 위로 내려앉았다. 휴일의 정적 속에서도 책상에 앉은 학생의 모습이 이곳의 진중함을 더욱 깊이 새겨주었다. 공부가 의무가 아닌 특권처럼 느껴지는 특별한 오후였다.

복도에 놓인 몇 대의 컴퓨터는 학생들을 비롯하여 필요한 경우에 관광객도 손쉽게 이용할 수 있겠다. 오픈된 서가에는 9백만 권 이상의 도서와 학술지 외에 지도, 영상 자료 등 방대한 자료를 소장하고 있어서 학생들에게 실질적 도움이 될 것이다.

1층 한쪽 벽에 사진과 설명으로 학교의 역사를 전시하고 있었다. 짧은 역사를 가진 미국은 역사를 아주 소중하게 대하고 있음을 이곳에서도 느낄 수 있었다. 대학교의 역사를 살펴보니 시간의 무게가 공간에 흐르고 있었다.

The moment I entered the Suzzallo and Allen libraries, I felt as if I had stepped into Hogwarts. Many people are mistaken, but this place has never filmed a Harry Potter movie before, and the inside of the library is similar, so it was enough to remind them of Hogwarts. The Gothic arches that soared toward the ceiling were magnificent and awe-inspiring. The sunlight coming in from the window sat down on the bookshelf. Even in the silence of the holiday, the image of the student sitting at the desk deeply engraved the seriousness of this place. It was a special afternoon when studying felt like a privilege, not an obligation.

There were some computers in the hallway that can be easily used by students and tourists when needed. In addition to more than 9 million books and academic journals, the open book house has a vast collection of materials such as maps and video materials, which will be of practical help to students.

On one wall on the first floor, the history of the school was displayed with photos and explanations. I could also feel here that the United States, which has a short history, treats history very dearly. Looking at the history of the university, the weight of time was flowing through the space.

도서관 입구에서는 졸업을 앞둔 여학생들이 기념사진을 찍고 있었다. 대학마다 졸업 가운이 다른지, 이 대학은 학사모와 가운 대신 보라색 어깨띠만 둘렀다. 하얀색 원피스 위에 보라색 어깨띠를 걸친 여학생들의 모습이 이지적이었다.

유럽 건축 양식을 모방하여 독특한 형태로 건축된 건물들이 조화롭게 어우러져 전체 대학 캠퍼스를 형성하고 있었다. 전통과 개성이 융합된 건물들이 대학을 한층 더 품격 있게 만들었다.

At the entrance of the library, female students who were about to graduate were taking commemorative photos. Universities have different graduation gowns, but the university only wore purple shoulder straps instead of academic hats and gowns. The appearance of female students wearing purple shoulder bands on white dresses was intellectual.

Buildings built in a unique form that imitated European architecture were harmoniously combined to form a university campus. Buildings that combine tradition and personality made the university more elegant.

아침에 보이지 않았던 레이니어산 꼭대기가 치솟는 분수 너머로 살포시 보였다. 역시 워싱턴주를 대표할 만한 산임을 부인할 수 없었다. 빙하가 더 녹지 않고 지금만큼이라도 산의 만년설이 지속되기를 빌었다.

계단을 따라 분수로 내려갔다. 분수 주변은 잘 가꿔진 잔디와 형형색색의 화단으로 꾸며져, 대학 건물을 한층 더 돋보이게 하였다. 가족 단위로 산책을 나온 사람들과 벤치에서 독서하는 학생들을 보니, 그 여유로움 속에 나도 스며들고 싶었다. 나와 말을 걸고 싶은 듯, 피하지도 않고 조용히 그 자리에 있는 오리는 나에게 잔잔한 위로가 되었다.

The top of Mount Rainier, which had not been seen in the morning, was glazed over the soaring fountain. Again, it could not be denied that it was a mountain that could represent Washington state. I hoped that the glaciers would not melt further and that the ice caps would continue as long as they are now.

I went down the stairs to the fountain. The area around the fountain was decorated with well-furnished grass and colorful flower beds, making the university building even more prominent. Seeing the people who came out for a walk as a family and the students reading on the bench, I wanted to permeate the relaxation. The duck, which seemed to want to talk to me and stayed there quietly without avoiding me, was a gentle comfort to me.

데이 호스트 로라와 만남

서바스 회원은 호스트와 데이 호스트로 나뉜다. 데이 호스트는 젊은 학생들처럼 집이 좁아서 재워줄 수 없는 상황이거나 개인적 사정으로 선택하는 경우이다. 잠을 재워주지 않는 대신 게스트에게 자기가 사는 지역을 안내하거나 식사를 같이하며, 문화와 경험을 공유한다.

점심을 대접하고 싶다던 데이 호스트 로라(Laura)와 연락하고 댁으로 갔다. 시애틀 부촌이라 불리는 머서 아일랜드(Mercere island)에 있었다. 호수가 보이는 근사한 곳에 위치한 회색 나무 벽으로 된 웅장한 이층집이었다. 1, 2층에 방이 여러 개, 화장실과 거실은 3곳이나 되었다. 무료인지는 모르겠으나 방 하나는 이탈리안 학생에게 렌트하였고, 한 곳에는 남자 친구가 가끔 와서 머문다고 하였다.

간단하게 차린 점심을 먹으며 그녀의 이야기를 들었다. 준비해 간 선물을 드리고, 집을 구경하였다.

Meeting with day host Laura

Servas members are divided into hosts and day hosts. Day hosts, like young students, are in situations where their homes are small and they cannot sleep or they choose for personal reasons. Instead of providing accommodation, they guide guests through their local area, share meals with them, and share culture and experiences.

I contacted the day host Laura, who wanted to treat me to lunch, and went her house. It was on Mercer Island, which is called Seattle's rich town. It was a grand two-story house with gray wooden walls, located in a wonderful location with a view of the lake. There were several rooms on the first and second floors, and three bathrooms and living rooms. I don't know if it's free, one room rented to Italian students, and I heard that her boyfriend sometimes comes and stays in one place.

I listened to her story over a simple lunch. I gave her some gifts and looked around the house with her.

젊은 시절, 남편과 자기가 했던 사업이 잘된 덕분에 플로리다에도 집을 소유하고 있었다. 여름에는 시애틀, 겨울에는 플로리다에 머문다고 하였다. 두 아들에서 태어난 손주들이 가끔 와서 그녀에게 생기를 더해주는 듯하였다. 우리가 방문했던 날 오후에도 손주가 와서 함께 보트를 탔다고 나중에 사진을 보내주었다.

건강했던 그녀의 남편은 14년 동안 암과 싸우면서도 마라톤을 했던 강인한 사람이었다. 그런 남편을 지켜보며 함께 견뎌낸 그녀에게 그의 죽음은 삶의 한 축이 무너지는 듯한 상실이었을 것이다. 배우자를 잃는 슬픔이 가장 크다고 하는데, 나는 그런 공허감과 슬픔이 얼마나 컸을지 상상조차 할 수 없었다. 몇 년 전부터 그녀가 다시 누군가를 향해 마음을 열었다니 다행이었다. 용기 있는 그녀를 진심으로 응원하고 싶다.

우리와 헤어지는 것이 섭섭한지 그녀는 우리가 차를 타고 떠날 때까지 오랫동안 우리를 배웅하였다.

She owned a house in Florida because, when she was young, her husband and her business went well. She said she would stay in Seattle in the summer and Florida in the winter. The grandchildren of the two sons sometimes came and seemed to add vitality to her. On the afternoon of our visit, her grandchild also came and sent me a picture later saying that they were on a boat together.

Her husband, who was healthy, was a strong man who ran marathons while fighting cancer for 14 years. For her, who endured with her husband while watching him, his death would have been a loss as if one of the pillars of her life were collapsing. It is said that the sadness of losing a spouse is the greatest, but I couldn't even imagine how great such emptiness and sadness must have been. I'm glad she opened her heart to someone again since a few years ago. I really want to support her with courage.

She saw us off for a long time until we left in the car, perhaps because she felt sad about breaking up with us.

시애틀 아울렛

로라 집에서 나와 시애틀 아울렛으로 갔다. 휴일이라서 얼마나 많은 사람이 쇼핑하러 왔는지 주차 자리가 거의 없었다. 2014년에 왔을 때 매우 싸게 샀던 기억을 더듬어 갔는데 우드번과 같은 가격으로 비쌌다. 딸이 원하는 가방을 찾지 못하고 밖으로 나왔다.

쇼핑 대신 “쇼핑의 즐거움, 행복한 발걸음”이라는 주제로 사람들의 모습을 카메라에 담았다. 아울렛의 거리를 가득 채운 사람들의 발걸음이 햇살에 흔들리는 쇼핑백처럼 가벼웠다. 연인이 사준 선물 보따리를 들고 다정하게 웃는 커플, 부모의 사랑이 담긴 신발 가방을 안고 달리는 아이. 이들을 바라만 보고 있어도 행복 바이러스가 전해오는 듯했다. 누구를 위해 산 상품인지 알 수 없지만 두 손을 꼭 잡고 걷는 부부의 모습이 오후의 햇살만큼 따뜻했다.

물건보다 마음이 오가는 풍경의 따스한 흐름을 카메라에 담았다. 사람들 손에 들린 것은 단지 하나의 물건이 아니라 서로를 향한 작은 배려와 사랑의 조각들이리라. 비록 쇼핑은 하지 못했으나 두 손 가득 선물을 받은 느낌이었다.

Seattle Outlet

I got out of Laura's house and went to a Seattle outlet. It was a holiday, there were few parking spots for how many people came to shop. When I came in 2014, I remembered buying it very cheaply, but it was expensive for the same price as Woodburn. I couldn't find the bag my daughter wanted and came out.

Instead of shopping, people were captured on camera under the theme of "The Joy of Shopping, Happy Steps." The steps of people filling the streets of the outlet were as light as shopping bags swaying in the sun. A couple who smiles affectionately with a bag of gifts their lovers bought for them, and a child who runs with a shoe bag containing their parents' love. Just looking at them, I felt like a happy virus was spreading. I don't know for whom they bought it, but the image of the some couple walking with their hands held tightly was as warm as the afternoon sun.

I took a picture the warm flow of the scenery, where hearts flow more than objects, on camera. It occurred to me that what was in people's hands was not just one object, but small pieces of consideration and love for each other. Even though I couldn't do anyshopping, I felt like I had received a handful of gifts.

집으로 돌아와 저녁을 준비하였다. 바바라 가족은 시애틀에 있는 한국 식당에 가서 가끔 외식하였다고 하였다. 불고기와 잡채가 주메뉴였다. 잡채를 먹은 경험이 있는데 쇠고기 전골은 처음이라고 하였다. 야들야들한 고기에 쇠고기 양념을 했으니 맛있는 냄새가 솔솔 풍겼다.

손님이 한 분 오시는 줄 알았는데 못 오신다고 하여서 못내 섭섭하였다. 가족들이 맛있게 먹어서 요리한 보람이 있었다. 식구라는 말처럼 함께 밥을 먹으니 더 가까워진 듯하였다.

I came back home and prepared dinner. The Barbara family went to a Korean restaurant in Seattle and sometimes ate out. Bulgogi and japchae were the main dishes. They said that they had eaten japchae before, but was their first time eating beef stew. The tender meat was seasoned with beef, so it smelled delicious.

I thought there was a guest coming, but I was disappointed that he couldn't come. It was worth cooking because the host family enjoyed it. As the saying goes, we are family, so we felt closer we ate together.

야경 산책

저녁을 먹고 브락 차를 타고 야경을 보러 나왔다. 도착한 노스 비치에 부드러운 바람이 스쳤다. 브락과 딸, 후배는 물새가 노는 모습을 지켜보는 동안, 나는 해안가에서 찰나의 풍경을 사진에 담았다.

날마다 하는 일상이 되었는지 산책 나온 어떤 개는 코스를 잘 알아 자기가 주인을 이끄는 것처럼 신바람이 났다. 나무에 걸린 해먹 속 누군가는 세상과 멀어진 듯 저무는 햇살에 녹아들고 있었다. 물속에서 퍼포먼스를 펼치고 금방 나온 여자는 축축한 머리카락을 쓰다듬으며 행복한 웃음을 지었다. 뭔가를 해냈다는 성취감이 그녀에게서 느껴졌으나 그 모습이 왠지 아름다우면서 슬펐다. 곳곳에 무리 지어 앉은 젊은이나 가족의 웃음을 보니 행복은 멀리 있는 것이 아니라 가까이에 있음을 다시 깨달았다.

A Walk to see the night view

After dinner, Brock drove out to see the night view. There was a gentle breeze on the arriving North Beach. While Brock, Eleanor and my junior watched the waterbird play, I took a picture of the momentary scene on the waterfront.

Perhaps it has become a daily routine, one dog that went out a walk knew the course well and seemed to be leading its owner with excitement. Someone in the hammock caught in the tree was melting in the sun as if they were far from the world. After performing in the water, the lady, who came out soon, stroked her wet hair and smiled happily. I felt a sense of accomplishment in her that she had accomplished something, but it was somehow beautiful and sad. When I saw the laughter of young people and their families sitting in groups everywhere, I realized again that happiness was not far away, but close.

해안가를 따라 걸었다. 어둑해진 바다 위, 잔잔한 파도가 일렁이는 틈 사이로 검은 실루엣이 조용히 모습을 드러내었다. 고요한 수면 위로 고개만 내민 물개 가족은 우두머리를 따라 어둠 속을 가로질렀다. 그들은 어디로 가는 것일까. 불안과 설렘을 안고 끝나지 않은 그들의 여정에, 파도가 마치 조심스럽게 배웅하는 듯하였다. 오래 살아왔던 현지인도 보기 드문 모습이라는데 그들을 본 우리는 행운이었다.

잔디밭에서 바렐(Barrel) 사우나라고 하는 이동식 통나무 찜질방을 보았다. 원형 구조라 열을 균일하게 순환시켜 효율적인 난방이 가능할 것 같았다. 장작 난방이라 환기를 위해 굴뚝이 설치되어 있었다. 실내 좌우에 배치된 벤치에 앉아서 땀을 낼 수 있겠다. 비가 많은 겨울철, 친구와 또는 연인끼리 뜨끈한 사우나에서 수다 떨고 몸을 데우며, 우울한 겨울을 이겨낼 수 있는 힐링 장소이리라.

I walked along the waterfront. A black silhouette appeared quietly on the darkened sea, through the gap between the calm waves. The seal family, who only raised their heads above the calm surface, followed the leader across the darkness. Where are they going? On their journey, which did not end with anxiety and excitement, the waves seemed to be carefully seen off. It is said that it is rare to see locals who have lived for a long time, and we were lucky to see them.

I saw a mobile log sauna called Barrel sauna on the lawn. it was a circular structure, it seemed that efficient heating would be possible by circulating heat uniformly. The chimney was installed for ventilation because it was wood heating. People can sit on benches placed on the left and right sides of the room and sweat. In the rainy winter, it will be a healing place where friends or lovers can chat and warm up in a hot mobile sauna, and overcome the gloomy winter.

시애틀 야경 장소 중에서 으뜸이라는 캐리 공원으로 갔다. 이미 많은 사람이 시애틀의 밤을 기다리며 자리를 잡고 있었다. 해가 떨어지자 도시는 푸른빛에 잠겼다. 도심을 대표하는 스페이스 니들은 무지개다리를 대신하여 하늘과 땅을 이어주는 듯했다.

워터프런트 주변의 불빛들이 바다로 부서졌다. 불빛을 품은 밤바다는 또 다른 하늘이 되었다. 야경에 취해 환호를 지르는 무리, 유쾌하게 웃는 소녀들, 조용히 구경하는 사람들, 모든 이들의 숨결마저도 별처럼 빛났다.

추위를 타는 엘레아노를 위해 집으로 돌아왔다. 미국 여행을 마무리하고 깊은 잠에 빠졌다.

We went to Carrie Park, which is the best place among Seattle night views. Many people were already sitting down waiting for the night in Seattle. As the sun went down, the city was overcast in blue. Space Needle, which represents the city center, seemed to connect the sky and the ground on behalf of the rainbow bridge.

The lights around the waterfront broke into the sea. The night sea with lights became another sky. Even everyone's breath shone like stars, the crowd of cheering in the night view, the girls laughing cheerfully, the quiet spectators.

We returned home for Eleanore who was cold. I finished my trip to the U.S. and fell into a deep sleep.

밴쿠버 아일랜드

Vancouver Island

국경을 넘어 밴쿠버섬으로

바바라 가족과 인사를 하고 차를 반납하러 갔다. 그들이 우리를 캐나다행 고속버스 정류소에 태워다 주기로 약속하고, 우리는 차를 빌렸다. 태워줄 사람이 없어서 우리를 바래다주지 못한다고 하니 명백하게 계약 위반인 셈이었다. 말다툼을 할 만큼 유창하게 영어를 잘했으면 따지고 택시비라도 받았을 텐데….

해외여행에서 가끔 차 렌트를 하였지만 이런 경우는 처음이었다. 다음에는 렌터카 계약에 이런 내용을 세세하게 적어야겠다. 그나마 계약할 때 담당했던 직원이 그들과 관련 있는 택시를 불러주어서 적당한 가격으로 고속버스 터미널에 갈 수 있었다. 남은 동전까지 탈탈 털어서 요금을 맞추어 주었다.

밴쿠버행 앞차를 놓치고 거의 두 시간을 기다려 1시 15분에 버스에 올랐다. 버스는 몇 곳에 멈추어 승객을 더 태웠다. 2014년에도 버스로 이곳을 통과하여 밴쿠버로 넘어갔었다. 코로나19를 지나면서 국경 심사가 더 강화된 듯했다. 버스에서 각자 짐을 찾아서 여권을 보여주며 이민국을 통과하였다. 다행히 버스 승객은 많지 않아 빠르게 진행되었다. 다시 짐을 버스 화물칸에 싣고, 버스에 올라 캐나다 영토에 들어섰다.

Cross the border to Vancouver Island

We said hello to Barbara's family and went to return the car. They promised to drop us off at the bus stop to Canada, so we rented a car. It was a clear violation of the contract to say that they couldn't escort us because they didn't have anyone to give us a ride. If I had been fluent enough to argue with English, I would have argued and even asked for taxi fare···.

I sometimes rent a car when I travel abroad, but this was the first time. Next time, I should write these details in the rental car contract. However, the employee in charge of the contract called a taxi related to them, so we was able to get to the express bus terminal at an affordable price. I paid for all the coins I had left.

I missed the car in front of Vancouver and waited almost two hours to get on the bus at 1:15. The bus stopped at a few places and picked up more passengers. I also took a bus through here in 2014 and went from the United States to Vancouver, Canada. As COVID-19 passed, border screening seemed to have strengthened. Each person found their luggage on the bus, showed his or her passport, and passed through the immigration office. Fortunately, there were not many bus passengers, so it proceeded quickly. I put my luggage back in the bus cargo hold, got on the bus, and entered Canadian territory.

창밖의 풍경은 점진적으로 변곡점을 맞이하였다. 미국과 사뭇 다른 풍광이 펼쳐졌다. 넓고 광활한 미국 고속도로 주변과 달리 덜 개발된 원시적인 자연이 보였다. 위도가 높아지면서 웅장하고 섬세한 곡선으로 이루어진 산맥의 나무들은 농밀한 초록빛으로 시선을 지배하였다. 공기마저 더 맑고 서늘하게 느껴졌다.

물리적인 경계를 넘어 서로 다른 미묘한 문화적 차이를 느끼다 보니 어느새 버스 종점 터미널에 도착하였다. 어디로 가야 하는지, 방향 감각이 사라졌다. 며칠 전의 일도 기억이 잘 나지 않는데, 10여 년 전에는 어디서 어떻게 갔는지 기억이 가물가물하였다.

구글 지도를 켜고 메트로역으로 갔다. 우여곡절 끝에 620번 버스를 타고 페리 터미널로 향하였다. 밴쿠버에서 츠와센으로 가는, 바다 위로 길게 뻗은 길은 막힘이 없었다. 반짝이는 윤슬이 바람에 흔들려 바다 위에서 은빛 비늘처럼 부서졌다.

The scenery outside the window gradually met an inflection point. The scenery was quite different from that of the United States. Unlike around the vast and huge U.S. highway, less developed primitive nature was seen. As the latitude increases, the trees of the mountain range, which consisted of magnificent and delicate curves, dominated the gaze with dense green light. Even the air felt clearer and cooler.

As I felt different subtle cultural differences across physical boundaries, and I arrived at the bus terminal. Where to go, I lost my sense of direction. I can't remember what happened a few days ago, and moreover, I couldn't remember where and how I went 10 years ago.

I turned on Google Maps and went to Metro Station. After many twists and turns, I took bus number 620 and headed to the ferry terminal. The journey from From Vancouver to Tsawwassen Ferry Terminal. the long stretch over the sea was unblocked. The twinkling ripples were shaken by the wind and broken like silver scales on the sea.

길 위를 지나가는 차들은 모두 같은 목적지로 가는 여행객들이리라. 제방 길을 달리는 동안은 일상의 소음과 잠시 멀어졌다. 멀리 보이는 항구의 크레인이 캐나다의 발전을 보여주듯 달리는 기린처럼 지나쳤다.

1959년 당시에 바다였던 곳을 막아서 2.5㎞ 제방을 쌓고, 그 위로 길을 내었다는 사실이 새삼 놀라웠다. 30분 넘게 달려 터미널에 도착하였다. 츠와센 페리 터미널은 캐나다 본토와 45개 섬 지역을 연결하는 해상 교통의 거점 기능을 하고 있었다.

호스트 수잔(Suzanne)과 연락을 종종 했음에도 불구하고 나는 목적지를 정확하게 인지하지 못하였다. 곧 출발하는가 싶었는데, 오후 7시까지 기다려야 하였다. 아침 일찍부터 설쳤는데도 불구하고, 차를 갈아타느라 점심을 먹지 못할 만큼 바쁜 하루였다.

배가 고파서 가게에서 샌드위치를 샀다. 진한 공감대가 느껴졌던 것일까. 일하는 동양계 아가씨가 딸 같아서 말을 걸었더니 워킹 홀리데이 2년 차인 한국인이었다. 일자리를 구하기 힘들어서 밴쿠버 서리에서 이곳까지 와서 일하고 있다고 하였다. 젊은이들이 좋은 일자리 찾기가 쉽지 않다는 것을 이곳에서도 여실히 보여주고 있었다. 그녀가 만든 신선하고 맛있는 샌드위치 맛을 보니 정성이 느껴졌다. 그녀의 앞날에 좋은 일과 성공이 가득하길 바란다는 응원을 해주었다.

All the cars passing by on the road are probably travelers going to the same destination. While running on the embankment road, I briefly moved away from the noise of everyday life. A crane in a port seen in the distance passed like a giraffe running as if showing Canada's development.

In 1959, it was surprising to build a 2.5㎞ embankment by blocking what was then the sea and to make a way on it. We ran for more than 30 minutes and arrived at the terminal. Tsawwassen Ferry Terminal served as a maritime transport hub connecting mainland Canada with 45 island areas.

Despite frequently contacting host Suzanne, I was not exactly aware of the destination I needed to get off. I thought it was leaving soon, but I had to wait until 7 p.m. It was a busy day, even though I started early in the morning, and I couldn't even eat lunch because I had to change vehicles.

I was hungry so I bought a sandwich at the store. Perhaps I felt a strong sense of same race. I spoke to a working Asian woman who seemed like my daughter, and she turned out to be a Korean who was in her second year of working holiday. She said she came here from Vancouver Surrey to work because it was difficult to find a job. Here too, I could feel that it is not easy for young people to find good jobs. I could feel her sincerity when I tasted the fresh and delicious sandwiches she made. I wished her a future filled with good things and success.

배는 움직이지 않는 듯 아주 천천히 나아갔다. 생각보다 바다 수면이 깊은지 가장자리를 따라가면서 섬의 근거리, 원거리 풍광을 보여주었다. 엎어지면 코 닿을 빤히 보이는 섬인데 1시간 30분이 걸렸다.

항구에 내리니 수잔이 나의 이름을 적은 종이를 들고 기다리고 있었다. 그녀의 작은 친절이 감동이었다. 그녀의 차는 캐리어 두 개가 들어가지 않을 만큼 작아서, 그녀의 남편 킷(Kit)도 트럭을 몰고 왔다. 나는 수잔 차에, 후배는 트럭에 타고 호스트 집으로 갔다. 수잔 집은 항구에서 약 15분 정도 떨어진 곳에 있었다. 한적한 오르막 도로에서 작은 사잇길로 들어가서 길 아래쪽에 있는 집은 자동차 문을 잠그지 않아도 될 정도로 안전한 곳이었다.

내가 건넨 선물 중에는 1만 원권을 넣어서 준비한 장지갑이 있었다. 지갑을 선물할 때는 돈을 넣어서 준다고 하니 우리 문화에 고개를 끄덕거리며 행복해하였다. 인사만 잠깐 하고, 수잔은 여행 기고를 쓴다고 밤늦게까지 작업을 하였다.

우리는 그녀 딸이 쓰던 방에서 묵었다. 딸은 마라톤에 참가했던 번호를 방문 위 벽에 다 붙여두었다. 보지 않았어도 건강했을 것 같다.

The ship moved very slowly, as if it was not moving. The sea surface was deeper than I thought, along the edge, showing the short-range and long-distance scenery of the island. It took an hour and a half for an island that you can see close to your nose when you fall down.

When I got off, Suzanne was waiting for me, holding a piece of paper with my name on it. Her small act of kindness really touched me. Her car was small enough to hold two carriers, so her husband Kit also drove a truck. I went to the host house in Suzanne's car and my junior in the truck. Suzanne's house was about 15 minutes away from the port. Entering a small side street from a quiet uphill road, the house down the street was safe enough not to have to lock the car door.

Among the gifts I gave was a long wallet prepared with 10,000 won bills in it. When I told her that when giving a wallet as a gift, she put money in it, she nodded happily in agreement with our culture. After a quick greeting, Suzanne stayed up late working on her travel article.

We stayed in the room her daughter used to use. Her daughter had the number she used to run the marathon posted on the wall above her room. I think she would have been healthy even if I hadn't seen her.

빅토리아 시내에서

버스를 타고 빅토리아 시내로 나갔다. 1999년도 여름에 처음 방문했었는데, 26년이 지난 지금도 국회의사당 주변은 건물이 조금 많아진 점을 제외하고는 많이 변하지 않아서 고마웠다. 하루가 다르게 변하는 세상살이에 적응하느라 힘겨운데, 급변하는 세상과 달리 느긋하게, 한 박자 늦게 사는 빅토리아 사람들이 부러웠다.

빅토리아 항구 끝자락에는 1898년에 완공된 우아하면서도 웅장한 모습의 국회의사당이 자리하고 있었다. 입구에는 빅토리아 여왕 동상이 이 섬을 지키듯 서 있었다. 왕관 모습의 푸른빛 돔은 유난히 반짝였고, 석벽은 오랜 세월의 이야기를 품은 듯 묵직하였다. 아치형 창문과 정교한 장식이 눈길을 붙잡고, 균형 잡힌 대칭미가 안도감을 더하였다.

한쪽에는 참전 용사를 위한 추모 동상이 서 있었다. 캐나다는 전쟁이 일어나는 곳곳에 참전하여 평화수호에 앞장섰다. 오로지 평화를 지키고, 한국을 돕겠다는 의지로 한국전쟁에 참전했을 터. 그들의 숭고한 정신에 숙연해졌다.

In downtown Victoria

I went out to downtown Victoria by bus. I visited for the first time in the summer of 1999, and I was grateful that 26 years later, the area around the BC Parliament Buildings remains almost unchanged. It was difficult to adjust to the changing world day by day, but unlike the rapidly changing world, I envied Victorians who lived a leisurely and one beat late.

At the end of Victoria Harbor was the elegant, magnificent BC Parliament Buildings, completed in 1898. At the entrance stood a statue of Queen Victoria as it guarded the island. The blue dome in the crown shape was particularly shiny, and the stone wall was heavy as if it had a story of many years. Arched windows and elaborate decorations caught the eye, and the balanced symmetry added relief.

On one side was a memorial statue for fallen war veterans. Canada stepped forward to uphold peace by taking part in conflicts wherever there was a war. They must have gone to war with nothing but the resolve to defend peace and to stand with Korea. protecting peace by sending troops to places where war broke out. I was filled with solemn reverence for their noble spirit.

계단을 내려가서 페리를 타는 곳으로 걸었다. 30년 넘게 이곳에서 그림을 그린다는 늙은 예술가의 소품을 한참 구경하였다. 빅토리아 항구의 모습이 잘 드러난 작은 그림을 하나 구입하였다.

캐나다라고 쓰인 구조물에 도착하기 전에 자그마한 키의 여인이 타일을 붙인 고래 형상물을 손질하고 있었다. 그녀의 어린 아들이 고래를 좋아하여 시의 허락을 받아 아들을 위해 그녀가 이곳에다 설치한 것이었다. 벌써 21년이 지났으니 타일 조각들이 떨어져서 보수하는 중이라고 하였다.

작품에 대한 그녀의 자부심과 함께 자신이 한 행동을 끝까지 책임지는 태도가 존경스러웠다. 우리나라에도 관공서나 호텔 등 큰 빌딩에 조각품들을 설치해 두었지만 이렇게 사후 관리 하는 것을 본 적이 없다. 관계자들이나 작품을 설치한 예술가들이 배워야 할 행동이 아닐까. 그녀의 아들 이름이 적힌 타일이 유난히 커 보였고, 하늘보다 더 푸른색으로 빛났다. 그녀로 인해 외관을 단장한 고래는 살아 움직이듯 생동감이 넘쳤다.

I walked down the stairs to the ferry offices. I've been looking at the props of an old painter who's been painting here for more than 30 years. I bought a small painting with a clear view of Victoria Harbor.

Before arriving at the structure written CANADA, a small woman was tiling a tiled whale figure. Her young son liked whales, so she set them up here for him with the permission of the city. Twenty-one years have already passed, and the tile pieces have fallen off and are being repaired.

I admired her pride in her work and her attitude of taking responsibility for what she did to the end. In Korea, sculptures have been installed in large buildings such as government offices and hotels, but I have never seen such follow-up management. Isn't it a behavior that officials and artists who installed the work should learn? The tile with her son's name looked extraordinarily large, and shone bluer than the sky. As a result of her, the beautifully decorated whale was alive and moving.

브리티시컬럼비아
왕립 박물관

밴쿠버섬은 남한의 1/3, 제주도 17배 크기이다. 남부, 서부, 중부, 북부, 내륙 등 다섯 구역으로 구분할 수 있다. 관광객 대부분은 남부에 속하는 빅토리아 지역에 몰려있는 대표적인 관광지만 구경하고 간다.

우리는 국회의사당 가까이 있는 브리티시컬럼비아 왕립 박물관에 먼저 들렀다. 박물관은 시간을 품은 집과 같았다. 기념품 가게 앞, 유리 진열장에 든 맘모스는 그 장소가 비좁은 듯 금방이라도 걸어나올 것 같았다. 발걸음을 조금 옮기면 원주민 조각상이 박물관을 지키듯 우뚝 서 있다.

작은 배를 타고 대서양을 건넜던 당시의 모습, 금광을 찾아 몰려들었던 개척 시대의 거리와 상점을 보고 있노라면 마치 19세기의 한복판에 들어선 듯하였다. 인도와 일본, 중국 등은 그때부터 이들과 교류하고 빨리 해외로 눈을 돌렸는데, 우리나라는 우물 안 개구리처럼 당파 싸움만 일삼았으니….

Royal Museum of British Columbia

Vancouver Island is one-third the size of South Korea and 17 times the size of Jeju Island. It can be divided into five districts: southern, western, central, northern, and inland. Most tourists visit only representative tourist attractions concentrated in Victoria, which belongs to the south.

We stopped by the Royal Museum of British Columbia near the Parliament Buildings. The museum was like a house holding time. The mammoth in the glass display case outside the souvenir shop looked ready to step out at any moment, as if the cramped space could barely contain it. With just a few step, a native Canadian statue tall as if guarding the museum.

Looking at the time when they crossed the Atlantic Ocean on a small boat, the streets and shops of the pioneering era that flocked to the gold mine, it seemed as if I had entered the middle of the 19th century. Since then, India, Japan, and China have interacted with them and quickly turned their eyes abroad, but Korea has only engaged in partisan fighting like a frog in a well….

왕립 박물관답게 19세기부터 근대까지 소장한 물건들이 많았다. 특히 귀한 옷감이나 옷들이 돋보였다. 200년 이상 되는 사진기도 눈길을 붙잡았다. 내가 저 시대에 태어났더라면, 어떤 나라에서 어떤 신분을 지닌 사람이었을까.

역사가 짧아서인지 캐나다 사람들은 역사를 정말 소중하게 여긴다. 그날, 박물관에 견학 온 학생들은 그들의 역사 한 줄이라도 빼먹지 않으려는 듯 교사의 설명에 귀를 쫑긋하여 경청하였다. 박물관 안 카페에서 간단히 점심을 먹고 밖으로 나왔다.

부차드 가든행 버스를 기다리는 동안 시티 투어용 마차에 눈길이 갔다. 말의 위생을 생각한 결정인지, 마부의 수고를 덜 작정이었는지, 관광객을 즐겁게 하려는 계산인지 알 수 없으나 말꼬리를 땋은 모습이 신선한 충격이었다.

As a royal museum, there have been many items that have been in the collection from the 19th century to the mordern period. In particular, precious fabrics and clothes stood out. A camera that is over 200 years old caught my eye. If I had been born in that era, what country would I have been in and what kind of status would I have had?

Perhaps because of their short history, Canadians really value history. On that day, the students who visited the museum listened intently to the teacher's explanation, as if they did not want to miss even a single line of their history. We had a simple lunch at a cafe in the museum and came out.

While I was waiting for the bus to Butchart Garden, I noticed the city tour wagon. I don't know if it was a decision considering the hygiene of the horse, whether it was intended to make the coach less laborious, or whether it was a calculation to entertain tourists, but the braided horse tail was a fresh shock.

부차드 가든

도심을 빠져나간 버스는 한적한 도로를 약 30분 달려 부차드 가든에 우리를 내려주었다. 매표소를 지나 안으로 들어가니 커다란 체스 판이 반겨주었다. 더 안쪽, 정원의 로고와 문구가 적힌 곳에서 인증 사진을 찍었다.

22헥타르 규모의 부차드 가든은 시멘트회사 사업가 로버트 피임 부차드(Robert Pim Butchart) 가문의 이름을 딴 정원이다. 1904년 남편이 채석장에서 석회석을 채굴한 황폐해진 땅을 부인이 직접 나무와 꽃을 심어 정원을 조성하기 시작하였다.

시멘트 채석장의 거칠고 황량한 땅이 꽃의 천국으로 변모할 줄 누가 상상했을까. 상처 입은 땅은 침몰 정원, 장미 정원, 일본 정원, 이탈리아 정원 등 하나하나 이름을 달리하여 완성되어 지금의 부차드 정원이 되었다.

Butchart Garden

After exiting the city center, the bus ran about half an hour down a quiet road and dropped us off at Butchart Garden. A large chessboard welcomed me when I went inside after passing through the ticket office. Inside, a certified photo was taken at a place with the garden's logo and words on it.

The 22-hectare Butchart Garden is named after the family of cement company entrepreneur Robert Pim Butchart. In 1904, his wife started to plant trees and flowers herself on the dilapidated land where her husband mined limestone in the quarry.

Who would have imagined that the rough and desolate land of the cement quarry would turn into a flower heaven? The damaged land was completed with different names, such as the sunken garden, rose garden, Japanese garden, and Italian garden, and became the current Butchart garden.

정원 곳곳에는 그곳 정원이 어떻게 탄생하였는지 초창기 사진을 곁들여 설명하였다. 본래 있던 연못과 절벽을 살리고, 물이 흐르던 곳과 들판을 활용하여 그에 맞는 정원을 꾸몄다. 자연을 크게 훼손하지 않고 최대한 본래 모습을 살려서 정원을 만들었기 때문에 길도 오르락내리락하였다. 장애인이 다닐 수 있는 길이 잘되어 있어서 휠체어를 미는 가족 단위의 관람객을 종종 보았다.

Throughout the garden, early photos of how the garden was created were explained. The original pond and cliff were saved, and the garden suitable for it was decorated using the water flowing and fields. The road went up and down because the garden was created by making the original appearance as much as possible without significantly damaging nature. The paths were well-maintained for disabled people, so I often saw families pushing wheelchairs.

잘 다듬어진 잔디는 부드러운 융단처럼 펼쳐졌고, 그 위에 우뚝 서 있는 키 큰 나무들은 한낮의 햇살을 적당히 걸러내며 길손에게 그늘을 내어주었다. 나무 사이로, 또는 돌담 사이에서 피어난 꽃들은 각기 다른 빛깔과 향기를 뽐내며 관람객을 붙잡아 세웠다.

활짝 핀 꽃을 배경으로 사진 찍는 젊은 여성은 꽃보다 더 환한 웃음을 남겼다. 꽃길 사이로 두 손을 꼭 잡고 천천히 걸음 걷는 노인들과 다정한 젊은 연인들의 손끝에는 꽃잎보다 더 은은한 온기가 담겨있을 듯하였다. 어린이들의 웃음소리는 분수의 물줄기와 뒤섞여 더 맑게 울려 퍼졌다. 관광객들의 행복이 곳곳에 스며들어 정원을 더 아름답게 만들었다.

The well-trimmed grass spread out like a soft carpet, the tall trees standing tall on it filtered out the midday sunlight and provided shade for travelers. Flowers blooming through trees or between stone walls attracted visitors, boasting different colors and scents.

A young woman taking pictures with flowers in full bloom as a background left a smile brighter than the flowers themselves. The fingertips of the elderly walking slowly, holding their hands tightly between the flower paths, and the young lovers walking affectionately seemed to contain a more subtle warmth than petals. The children's laughter was mixed with the fountain's stream of water and resonated clearer. The happiness of tourists permeates every corner, making the garden even more beautiful.

폐장 시간에 맞추어 나오느라 잠깐 마주한 이탈리안 정원은 오랫동안 잊을 수 없을 것 같았다. 마치 베르사유 정원의 한 부분처럼, 깔끔하게 다듬어진 나무 사이에 난 하얀 아치문으로 금방이라도 요정이 나타날 것만 같았다. 바로 앞에 핑크빛 꽃으로 장식된 작은 연못과 창문을 제외하고 아이비 덩굴로 뒤덮인 건물은 온통 초록으로 관광객들을 매료시켰다.

정원의 아름다움을 뒤로하고 우리를 데리러 온 킷(Kit)의 차를 타고 집으로 왔다. 외국 서바스 가족 대부분은 남편들이 요리를 잘했다. 요리 솜씨가 좋은 어머니의 영향을 받았다는 킷도 예외는 아니었다.

대구를 오븐에 구운 후에 다시 프라이팬에서 구운 생선 요리는 어디서도 먹어보지 못한 독특한 맛이었다. 정성이 들어간 생선은 별다른 반찬이 없어도, 찰기 없는 밥맛을 커버해 주었다.

The Italian garden, which I briefly encountered in time for closing, seemed unforgettable for a long time. Like a part of the Versailles garden, a fairy appeared at any moment through a white arch door between neatly trimmed trees. A small pond decorated with pink flowers right in front of it, and a building covered with green ivy vines, except for windows, fascinated tourists.

Leaving the beauty of the garden behind, Kit's car came home to pick us up. Most of the foreign Servas family members were good cooks by their husbands. Kit, who was influenced by his mother, who was a good chef.

After roasting cod in the oven, the fish dish baked in a frying pan was a unique taste that I had never eaten anywhere else. The fish with sincerity covered the taste of rice without stickiness and no side dishes.

저녁 식사를 마치고 수잔이 일몰을 보고 싶다는 우리를 태우고 바닷가로 데려갔다. 다대포나 해운대처럼 모래사장이 펼쳐진 해안을 기대했으나 도로에서 태평양으로 곧장 이어진 깊은 바다였다. 빅토리아가 태평양에 위치한 섬이란 것을 잊고 있었다. 당연하다고 생각한 한국의 바닷가들이 훨씬 예쁘고 아기자기하다는 것을 다시 알게 되었다. 탁 트인 바다는 웅장했지만, 한국의 해안가에서 느낄 수 있는 포근함이나 익숙한 정취는 없었다.

나는 일몰 찍을 준비를 하였고, 후배와 수잔은 바닷가 주변을 걸었다. 거세게 부는 바람에 카메라 받침대가 흔들렸고, 나 역시 바람에 휘청였다. 붉고 장엄한 석양을 기대했으나 태양은 어둡고 두꺼운 구름 사이로 겨우 가느다란 빛을 남기고 사라졌다. 은은한 노을이 아닌 바람과 먹구름이 가득한 낯선 일몰로 기억될 것 같다.

After dinner, Suzanne us to the beach when we wanted to see the sunset. I expected a beach with open sandy beaches like Dadaepo or Haeundae, but it was a deep sea that led directly from the road to the Pacific Ocean. I forgot that Victoria is an island located in the Pacific Ocean. I learned again that the beaches of Korea that I took for granted are much prettier and cute. The open sea was magnificent, but there was no warmth or familiar atmosphere that could be felt on the coast of Korea.

I was ready to shoot the sunset, and my junior and Suzanne walked around the beach. The camera pedestal was shaken by the strong wind, and I was also reeling by the wind. I expected a red and majestic sunset, but the sun disappeared barely through the dark and thick clouds. I think it will be remembered as an unfamiliar sunset filled with wind and dark clouds, not a gentle sunset.

생명의 춤을 추는 보타니컬 해안

아침 식사 전에 정원을 둘러보았다. 작은 연못과 텃밭도 있었고, 과일나무와 여러 가지 꽃들이 서로 뽐내고 있었다. 아침 햇살이 좋아서 야외에서 아침을 먹었다. 집에서도 서양식으로 간단히 아침을 먹는데, 수잔이 챙겨준 아침이 좀 더 특별하였다. 몇 가지 유기농 곡류를 밤새 우유에 불렸다가 아침에 과일 몇 조각과 견과류를 조금 넣어서 먹었다. 영양가나 포만감으로 충분한 한 끼 식사가 되었다.

다 먹고 안으로 들어오니 이름 모를 새가 날아와서 두리번거리다가 재빨리 모이주머니를 쪼아대었다. 아침 일찍 내가 새의 식사를 방해한 것은 아닐까. 길거리 나무에 새집을 달아두거나 집 발코니에 먹이 주머니를 달아두는 등 동물과 함께 살아가는 캐나다 사람들이 존경스러웠다. 다시 보지 못할 순간의 포착이 평화스러운 풍경으로 각인되었다.

Botanical Coast, where life dances

I looked around the garden before breakfast. There was also a small pond and a garden, and fruit trees and various flowers were showing off each other. I had breakfast outside because the morning sun was nice. I ate a simple Western-style breakfast at home, but the breakfast Suzanne prepares was a little more special. I soaked some organic grains in milk overnight and ate them with a few pieces of fruit and some nuts in the morning. It was a good meal with nutritional value or satiety.

When I finished eating and came inside, an unknown bird flew in, looked around, and quickly pecked at the feed bag. Maybe I interrupted the bird's diet early in the morning. Canadians living with animals, such as hanging bird houses on roadside trees or hanging food bags on the balcony of their houses, were respected. The capture of a moment that will never be seen again was imprinted as peaceful.

아침을 먹고 킷이 공항 근처 렌터카 업체에 데려다주었다. 우리끼리 갔으면 사무실이 옮긴 곳을 몰라 헤매었을 텐데, 덕분에 수월하게 차를 빌릴 수 있었다.

목적지는 보타니컬 비치였다. 빗방울 자국이 남은 도로 옆, 나비 떼 같은 금작화가 길을 안내하였다. 도로와 언덕을 따라 길게 이어진 노란 물결은 회색 하늘과 대조되어 황금빛으로 선명하게 빛났다. 노란 길이 끝나고 쭉쭉 뻗은 전나무와 삼나무가 빼곡한 길로 들어서니 다른 공기가 흘렀다. 눈에 보이지 않는 작은 입자들이 자동차의 열린 창으로 들어와 나의 폐부까지 맑게 바꿔주었다.

보타니컬 비치는 후안 드 푸카 주립공원 안에 있는 바닷가이다. 물때를 보지 않고 찾아갔는데, 다행히 물이 빠진 시간이라서 제대로 해안 풍광을 즐길 수가 있었다.

After breakfast, Kit took us to a rental car company near the airport. If we had gone on our own, we would have wandered around not knowing where the rental car company moved, but thanks to this, we could easily rent a car.

The destination was Botanical Beach. Next to the road with raindrops marks, Broom flowers like a flock of butterflies guided the road. The long yellow waves along the roads and hills contrasted with the gray sky and shone clearly in golden light. After the yellow road was over, the stretched fir and cedar trees entered the packed road, and a different air flowed. Small invisible particles entered the car's open window and changed my lung area to be clear.

Botanical Beach is a beach within Juan de Fuca Provincial Park. I went there without looking at the draining time, but fortunately, it was a time when the water was drained, so we were able to enjoy the coastal scenery properly.

주차장에서 한참을 걸어 내려가는 숲길은 사람들의 손길이 많이 닿지 않아 나무는 제멋대로 자라고 있었다. 태평양의 거친 숨결이 머문 해안은 전혀 예상하지 못한 풍경으로 우리를 맞이하였다.

바다 가까이 납작 엎드린 바위는 오랜 세월 동안 켜켜이 쌓인 층과 파도에 깎이고 파인 결이 선명하게 드러났다. 곳곳에 생긴 조수 웅덩이에는 오색찬란한 생명의 향연이 펼쳐졌다. 보석처럼 빛나는 말미잘이 촉수를 흔들며 춤추고, 구멍 안에는 생전 처음 보는 보랏빛 성게가 터줏대감처럼 한 자리씩 차지하고 있었다. 바위 끝에 달린 홍합과 따개비, 그들을 먹으러 움직이는 불가사리 등 저마다 고유한 생존의 방식을 보여주었다.

숲과 연결된 깎인 절벽 역시 파도의 날 선 흔적을 품고 있었다. 가로로 그림을 그린 듯, 쐐기나 끌로 돌을 떼어낸 듯 다른 모습으로 자연은 벽화를 만들었다.

단순한 해안이 아니라 시간과 파도가 빚어낸 예술 작품이었고, 수많은 생명이 어우러져 춤을 추는 장엄한 무대였다. 또한 대자연이 펼쳐놓은 한 권의 지질학적 시와도 같았다. 살아있는 모든 것이 제자리에서 빛나는 곳, 생명의 끈질긴 의지를 보여주는 숭고한 해안이었다.

The forest path leading down from the parking lot was untouched by humans, so the trees were growing wildly. The coast, where the rough breath of the Pacific Ocean lingered, welcomed us with a completely unexpected landscape.

On the rock lying flat near the sea, clearly shows the layers of sand that have accumulated over many years and the winkles that have been eroded by waves. A colorful feast of life was spread out in the tidal pools everywhere. A jewel-like sea anemone danced with its tentacles, and a purple sea urchin, which I had never seen in my life, occupied the hole one by one like a turtleneck. Each of them showed their own way of survival, such as mussels and barnacles at the end of the rock, and starfish that moved to eat them.

The carved cliffs connected to the forest also contained traces of the wave's edge. Nature created murals in a different way, as if drawing horizontally, as if the stones were removed with a wedge or chisel.

It was not just a beach, but a work of art created by time and waves, and it was a majestic stage where countless lives danced together. It was also like a geological poem spread out by Mother Nature. Where everything that is alive shines in place, it was a sublime beach that showed the persistent will of life.

밴쿠버

Vancouver

마지막 여정, 밴쿠버로

아침 식사 후 수잔이 우리를 항구까지 바래다주었다. 며칠 지냈다고 항구까지 가는 길이 낯설지 않았다. 출항 시각을 알고 출발하였기에 여유롭게 9시 배를 탈 수 있었다.

밴쿠버에서 들어올 때와 반대로 배는 섬의 평화로운 모습을 보여주며 천천히 나아갔다. 배에서 내려서, 버스를 타고 시내에 진입하기 전에 우연히 공사 현장을 보았다. 다시 밴쿠버를 방문했을 때, 이 주변이 어떻게 변했을지 궁금해졌다. 자연을 덜 훼손하면 좋겠다는 혼자만의 소원을 빌었다.

The last journey, to Vancouver

After breakfast, Suzanne drove us to the port. Having stayed here for a few days, the route to the port felt familiar. I was able to take the ship at 9 o'clock leisurely because I left after knowing the time of departure.

The ship moved slowly, showing the peaceful appearance of the island, as opposed to when it came in from Vancouver. After getting off the ship, I happened to see the construction area before taking the bus into town. When I visited Vancouver again, I wondered how the surroundings here would have changed. I made my own wish that it would be better to damage nature less.

버스에서 내려 다시 전차와 버스로 갈아타고, 호스트 모니카와 존의 집에 도착하였다. 그들의 집은 밴쿠버 대학교 근처에 있었다. 버스에서 내려 집까지 걷는데 가로수가 우거졌고, 다람쥐도 보여서 마치 공원을 걷는 것 같았다.

바깥에서 보면 2층, 뒤뜰에서 보면 3층인 집이다. 부부 내외는 외출 중이라 집에 있던 장녀가 문을 열어주었다. 짐만 집 안에 두고 우리는 시내로 나왔다. 가는 도중에 섬에서는 볼 수 없었던 경찰차가 보였고, 대도시답게 도로가 복잡하였다.

I got off the bus, switched to the train and bus again, and arrived at host Monica and John's house. Their house was near the University of British Columbia. When I got off the bus and walked home, the street trees were thick and I saw squirrels, so it was like walking in a park.

From the outside, it is a two-story house and from the backyard, it is a three-story house. Monica and her husband, John were out, so their eldest daughter, who was at home, opened the door. We left our luggage in the house and went downtown. On the way, I saw a police car that was not seen on the island, and the road was complicated like a big city.

여전한 밴쿠버 시내

밴쿠버는 세 번째 방문하는 도시이다. 시내는 유리와 철골로 만들어진 고층 빌딩이 이전보다 더 높이 솟아서 마치 새로운 얼굴을 보여주는 듯하였다. 유리 벽에 반사된 햇빛이 거리를 한층 밝게 비추었다. 칙칙한 건물 사이에서 화려한 건물 벽화가 꽃처럼 피어났다. 전차와 버스들이 승객을 실어 나르느라 바쁘게 이동하였다.

개스타운에 들어서니 시간이 멈춘 듯하였다. 1977년에 세워진 증기 시계는 여전히 시각에 맞춰 김을 내뿜었고, 그 모습을 지켜본 관광객들은 감탄을 아끼지 않았다. 사람들의 웃음소리와 사진기 셔터 소리, 행위예술자로 인해 골목이 활기찼다. 길가에 늘어선 기념품 가게 안, 붐비는 여행자 속으로 우리도 끼어들었다. 도시는 빠르게 모습을 바꾸었으나 개스타운은 마치 오래된 책갈피처럼 제자리를 지키며 사람들을 반겨주었다.

Downtown Vancouver as ever

I am visiting Vancouver for the third time. In the city, high-rise buildings made of glass and steel frame soared higher than before, as if showing a new face. The sunlight reflected off the glass walls brightened the street. Gorgeous building murals bloomed like a flower among the dull buildings. Trams and buses were busy carrying passengers.

Time seemed to have stopped when I entered Gastown. The steam clock, which was built in 1977, still steamed in time, and the tourists who watched it admired. The alley was lively due to people's laughter, camera shutters, and performance artists. We also stepped into the crowded travelers in the souvenir shops lined the side of the road. In the city center, which quickly changed its appereance, but Gastown welcomed people, staying in place like an old bookmark.

302
OLDE TYME
CANDY
SHOPPE
I
ACTIVATE
DONATION

STEAMWORKS
BREWERY PUB RESTAURANT
STEA
Public Washroom

밴쿠버 중앙 도서관

해외여행 중에 시장과 도서관에 꼭 들르곤 한다. 시장에 가면 사람들의 일상과 생생한 삶의 현장을 느낄 수가 있다. 현지 음식을 맛보고, 흥정하는 소리와 언어를 생생히 들을 수 있다. 물건 파는 사람들의 표정에서 그곳의 생활 수준을 빨리 파악하게 된다. 관광지와는 다른 진짜 얼굴을 만날 수 있다.

도서관은 그 도시의 사고방식과 문화를 엿볼 수 있는 곳이다. 건물은 어떤지, 어떤 책이 꽂혀 있는지, 사람들이 어떻게 시간을 보내는지 볼 수 있다. 그 사회가 지향하는 가치와 생활 리듬을 알 수 있는 곳이다.

밴쿠버 중앙 도서관으로 가는 길에서 알코올과 약물에 기대어 하루를 버티는 사람들을 마주하였다. 그들의 눈빛은 닿지 못할 허공으로 향하고, 자기 몸도 제대로 가누지 못한 상태로 공원 여기저기에 널브러져 있었다. 복잡하게 뒤얽힌 전깃줄처럼 그들의 인생은 언제부터, 왜 저렇게 꼬이기 시작했을까. 나는 알 수 없는 무거운 발걸음을 옮겼다.

책의 향기와 지성을 상징하는 도서관 건물과 삶의 끝자락에서 흔들리는 사람들이 불과 몇 걸음 사이에 놓여 있었다. 화려함과 고통이 공존하는 도시, 비단 밴쿠버만의 문제는 아니었다. 세계 유명 도시라 일컫는 뉴욕, 파리, 스톡홀름, 시드니 등, 심지어 모로코의 어느 도시에서도 마약중독자들을 마주하였다. 우리나라도 더 이상 마약 안전지대가 아니다. 평범한 주부와 어린 학생들까지 시나브로 빠져들고 있는 현실이다.

여행은 결국, 아름다움만 아니라 그곳의 모순과 어두운 그림자까지 마주하는 일이다.

Vancouver Central Library

When I travel abroad, I always visit the market and the library. If I go to the market, I can feel people's daily lives and vivid scenes of life. I can taste local food and hear the sound and language of bargaining vividly. I can quickly grasp the standard of living there from the expressions of the people selling goods. I can meet a real faces different from a tourist destination.

The library is a place where you can get a glimpse of the city's mindset and culture. You can see what the building is like, what books are there, and how people spend their time. It is a place where you can see the values and rhythms of life that the society aims for.

On the way to the Vancouver Central Library, I faced people who endured the day leaning on alcohol and drugs. There were some people whose eyes were facing somewhere far away and out od reach. They were moving erratically all over the park, unable to even control his body. When and why did their lives get twisted like that, like electric lines intricately entangled between soaring buildings? I took a heavy unknown step.

The library building, symbolizing the scent and intelligence of the book, even while people, swaying at the end of their lives, lay just a few steps away. Vancouver is not just a problem in a city where glamour and pain co-exist. Some of the world's most famous cities, such as New York, Paris, Stockholm, Sydney, and even any other city in Morocco, have faced drug addiction. Even our country is no longer a drug safe zone. Even ordinary housewives and young students are slowly falling in.

After all, travel is not only about beauty, but also about the contradictions and dark shadows there.

밴쿠버 중앙 도서관은 로마의 콜로세움을 연상시켰다. 거대한 원형 벽으로 둘러싸인 미로 같아서 한참 동안 입구를 찾아다녔다. 도서관인지 백화점인지 모를 정도로 1층에는 부동산, 미용실, 카페 등 상점이 즐비하였다.

도서관 안으로 들어서는 순간, 마치 숨겨둔 아지트에 발을 들여놓은 듯하였다. 가장 먼저 나를 반겨준 햇살은 천장 끝에서 바닥까지 이어진 유리벽 사이로 따뜻하게 퍼졌다. 2층부터 7층까지 책이 꽂힌 모든 서가는 오픈이다. 필요한 책을 찾아 창가에 놓인 열람석에서 책을 읽을 수 있다. 책장을 넘기는 손끝 너머로 빌딩 숲과 파란 하늘이 이어진다.

The Vancouver Central Library was built to resemble of the Colosseum of Rome. It was like a maze surrounded by huge circular walls, so I looked for the entrance for a long time. There were so many shops, such as real estate, hair salons, and cafes on the first floor, that it was not known whether it was a library or a department store.

As soon as I entered the library, it was as if I had stepped into a hidden hideout. The sunlight that greeted me first spread warmly through the glass walls that stretched from the end of the ceiling to the floor. All bookshelves with books from the second floor to the seventh floor are open. You can find the books you need and read them in the reading room by the window. A forest of buildings and a blue sky continue like fingertips over the bookshelf.

누구나 이용 가능한 컴퓨터가 있는 공간은 꽤 넓어서 원하는 것을 검색하거나 영화, 게임 등을 마음대로 하고 있었다. 이 도서관에서 가장 인상 적인 곳은 정원이 있는 옥상이었다.

옥상에서 바라본 구름이 드리워진 하늘은 더없이 파랬고, 돛을 연상시키는 캐나다 플레이스의 지붕을 보니 크루즈를 타고 알래스카로 떠나는 모습을 꿈꾸게 하였다. 책을 읽다 잠깐 쉬고 싶을 때 옥상에 오르면, 바람은 너의 머릿결을 만지고, 긴 호흡을 줄 거야.

도서관은 책을 읽거나 빌리는 곳만이 아니라, 시간을 잠시 멈추어 나를 들여다보게 하는 공간이었다. 책의 숲이자 빛의 광장으로, 시민들의 멋진 휴식처가 되어주었다.

The space with a computer available to anyone is quite large, so many people were searching for what they wanted or were playing movies, games, etc. The most impressive place was rooftop garden.

The cloud-covered sky seen from the rooftop was incredibly blue, the sail-like roof of Canada Place made me dream of taking a cruise to Alaska. If you climb to the rooftop when you want to take a break while reading a book, the wind will brush your hair and give you a long breath.

The library was not just a place to read or borrow books, but a space that paused time to look into myself. It was a forest of books and a plaza of light, making it a wonderful resting place for citizens.

모니카 댁으로

호스트 집에 거의 다 왔을 때, 채소밭에 물 주는 한국 아저씨를 만났다. 아들 유학 때문에 밴쿠버로 왕래하다가 이민 간 지 15년 정도 된 분이었다. 이런 곳에서 한국인, 그것도 경상도 분을 만나니 더욱 반가웠다. 그분에게 서바스를 소개해 주고, 집으로 오니 모니카와 존이 반겨주었다.

처음에 도착했을 때는 주인이 없어서 집 안을 자세히 살펴보지 못하였다. 반지하에 막내딸이 독립적으로 살고 있었다. 현관에서 왼쪽으로 거실, 식탁, 부엌으로 이어졌고, 오른쪽은 우리가 묵었던 큰방과 화장실이 있었다. 2층에 화장실 2개와 방이 5개, 입구 열린 공간에 세탁실이 있었다.

내가 호스트를 위해 준비한 마지막 선물 보따리 속에는 모니카의 손녀를 위한 진짜 한복이 있었다. 손녀는 다른 곳에 살아서 우리가 밴쿠버에 머무는 동안에 만나지 못했다. 모니카는 손녀가 한복 입은 모습을 한참 뒤, 9월에 보내주었다.

To Monica's house

When I was almost at the host's house, I met a Korean man who was watering his vegetable garden. He had immigrated to Vancouver about 15 years ago because of his son's study abroad. It was very nice to meet Koreans, especially Gyeongsang-do, in this place. I introduced him to Servas, and when I came home, Monica and John welcomed me.

When I first arrived, I couldn't take a closer look at the house because there was no owner. Her eldest daughter lived independently in the semi-basement. From the front door to the left, it led to the living room, dining room, and kitchen, and on the right, there was a bathroom when I went out of the large room I stayed in. There were five rooms on the second floor, including two bathrooms and a laundry in an open space.

In the last package of gifts I brought for our host was a real hanbok for their granddaughter. Unfortunately, their granddaughter lived somewhere else, so I couldn't meet her, while we were in Vancouver. Monica sent a picture of her granddaughter wearing the hanbok in September, a long time later.

모니카가 요리한 미트볼과 샐러드, 빵이 저녁 식사였다. 우리가 매일 밥을 먹듯이 평범한 식사이리라. 비타민을 보충이라도 하듯이 다양한 채소가 반가워서 샐러드를 너무 많이 먹었다. 디저트로 아이스크림까지 먹었다.

모니카에게 호스트를 요청할 때 그녀는 유럽 여행 중이라서 남편 존이 답을 주었다. 호스트 허락에 대한 감사 인사로 말문을 열었다. 사업과 여행 겸 다녀온 모니카의 유럽 이야기를 듣고, 우리가 오늘 이동한 이야기와 시내에서 있었던 일들을 이야기하며 하루를 마무리하였다.

Dinner was meatballs, salad and bread cooked by Monica. It must be a normal meal for them like we eat every day rice. I ate too much salad because I was glad to see various vegetables for vitamin supplementation. I even ate ice cream for dessert.

When I asked Monica to host, she was traveling to Europe, so her husband, John, gave me an answer. I opened my speech by thanking her for the host's permission. After listening to Monica's story in Europe, which holiday trip, we talked about the stories of our traveling and what happened in the city today. Then we finished the day.

마을 산책

아침부터 비가 내렸다. 어제 약속한 것을 지키기 위해 우리는 우산을 쓰고, 비옷을 입은 모니카를 따라 산책에 나섰다. 숲으로 가는 도중에, 모니카의 지인 집의 문을 열어서 우리에게 작은 말을 보여주었다. 마당이 넓지도 않은 집에서 어떻게 당나귀를 키울 수 있을까 궁금해졌다.

집에서 몇 블록을 지나 밴쿠버대학까지 이어지는 숲길 입구에 도착하였다. 비가 내리는데도 아랑곳하지 않고 달리는 사람들이 종종 보였고, 반려견을 산책시키기 위해 나온 사람들도 많았다. 반려견을 키우는 사람들은 부지런하지 않으면 안 될 것 같다.

슈퍼마켓으로 가는 길에 그물망을 두른 나무를 보았다. 집을 짓거나 공사할 때, 나무 근처에 자재나 폐기물을 두지 않도록 나무를 보호하기 위해서란다. 캐나다인이 얼마나 자연을 보호하는지 알 수 있었다.

Walking to village

It had been raining since the morning. To keep our promise of yesterday, we used umbrellas, and went for a walk with Monica wearing her raincoat. On the way to the forest, Monica opened the secret door of an acquaintance's house, and showed us the small horse. I wondered how they could raise a horse in a house that didn't even have a large yard.

After two blocks from her house, we arrived at the entrance to the forest path that leads to the University of British Columbia. I often saw people running regardless of the rain, and many came out to walk their dogs. People who raise dogs seem to have to be diligent.

On my way to the supermarket, I saw a tree with a mesh around it. This is to protect trees when building or constructing houses nearby. I could see how much Canadians protect nature.

미국이나 캐나다의 슈퍼마켓을 가면 입구부터 기분이 좋다. 입구에 있는 화분과 꽃들이 싱그러운 향기와 화사한 색으로 반겨주니 발걸음이 한결 가벼워진다. 철마다 다른 아름다운 꽃을 피워 고객들의 눈길을 사로잡는다. 꽃집이나 슈퍼, 양쪽에게 다 좋은 상술이다.

우리가 갔던 슈퍼는 제법 컸다. 진열대 사이를 걷다 보니 익숙한 한국 제품들이 가득 진열되어 있었다. 라면과 다양한 과자들과 소스까지. 먼 곳에서 마주한 익숙한 포장지들은 고향의 손길을 만난 듯 괜히 마음이 든든해졌다. 미국 제품은 관세 탓인지 내가 원하는 쿠키들이 없었으나 그 빈자리는 허전하지 않았다. 오히려 그 자리를 차지한 한국 제품의 존재감이 더욱 빛났다. 장바구니에 담는 순간은 단순히 물건을 고르는 일이 아니라, 낯선 도시 속에서 내 삶의 조각을 다시 만나는 경험이었다.

When I go to supermarkets in the United States or Canada, I feel good from the entrance. The flower pots and flowers at the entrance welcome the fresh scent and bright color, making my steps lighter. It catches customers' eyes by blooming beautiful flowers different from season to season. It is a good tactic for both florists and supermarkets.

The supermarket I went to was quite big. Walking between the shelves, I found a full display of familiar Korean products, including ramen, and various snacks and sauces. Seeing familiar wrappers that I encountered from far away, I felt reassured as if I had met my hometown's touch. The U.S. product did not have the cookies I wanted, perhaps due to tariffs, but the vacancy was not empty. Rather, the presence of Korean made the place was more prominent. Shopping was not just about choosing things, it was an experience of meeting pieces of my life again in an unfamiliar city.

나 혼자 동네 한 바퀴

집으로 돌아올 때부터 힘이 없고, 속이 불편했다. 어제 점심때 베트남 국수를 먹을 때부터 속이 안 좋았는데 억지로 먹은 것이 후회스러웠다. 어제 저녁 식사도 맛있다고 다른 날보다 많이 먹은 것이 원인이었다. 아침을 굶고 전기 매트를 켜서 배를 깔고 한숨 자고 나니 좀 나아졌다.

후배는 모니카의 친구, 마리와 함께 외출하고 집에 없었다. 나 혼자 동네로 나갔다. 멀리 가지 않았는데도 매끈하게 다듬어진 잔디를 가진 집들이 눈에 띄었다. 잔디가 보내는 푸른빛이 동네 전체를 한결 고급스럽고, 안정된 느낌으로 만들었다.

길을 따라 걸으니 작은 사립 초등학교가 있었다. 교회 재단이라서 그런지 건물이 성스럽게 보였고, 소박하면서도 따뜻한 분위기가 풍겼다. 음악 소리를 따라가니 학교 기금 마련을 위한 행사를 하고 있었다. 우리나라는 학교나 지자체 주최로 프로그램을 구성하여 축제를 연다. 반면 이곳에는 학생과 학부모가 주관하여 프로그램을 만들기 때문에 온 가족이 참여하고, 한 부분이라도 맡아서 행사를 이끌었다.

I'll go around the neighborhood by myself

After returning to host house, I felt weak and my stomach was uncomfortable. I felt sick since I ate Vietnamese noodles at lunch yesterday. I regret that I forced myself to eat it. Yesterday's dinner was also delicious, and it was because I ate more than other days. I felt better after skipping breakfast and sleeping on an electric mat.

My junior went out with Monica's friend Mary and wasn't home, so I went out to the neighborhood by myself. Even though I didn't go far, houses with smooth trimmed grass stood out. The green color sent by the grass made the whole neighborhood feel more luxurious and stable.

Walking along the road, there was a small private elementary school. Perhaps because it was a church foundation, the building looked sacred, and it had a simple yet warm atmosphere. Following the sound of the music, there was an event to raise funds for the school. Korea holds a festival by organizing programs hosted by schools or local governments. On the other hand, since the program was organized by students and parents, the whole family participated and led the event by taking care of a part.

음식을 준비하고, 소시지를 굽고, 테이블 정리 등에 많은 학부형이 참여하였다. 동네 주민들이 회원인 밴드는 요란하지 않으나 열정적으로 연주하였다. 한 코너에서는 학생이 쿠폰을 받으면서 아이들의 낚시 게임을 책임졌고, 야외 잔디밭에서는 토끼 먹이를 팔면서 토끼를 만지도록 허락하였다. 교회 안에서는 주민들의 그림이나 사진 등 작품을 전시, 판매 중이었다. 학교, 교회, 마을 사람들이 지역 공동체로 함께 살아가는 모습이 부러웠다.

Many parents participated in preparing food, baking sausages, and organizing tables. The band which was comprise of local residents, played enthusiastically, not loudly. In one corner, a student was responsible for children's fishing games while receiving coupons, and in the outdoor lawn, they were allowed to touch rabbits while selling rabbit food. Inside the church, works such as paintings and photographs of residents were displayed and sold. I was envious of the school, church, and village people living together as a local community.

아침에 갔던 길을 기억하며 숲 입구로 걸었다. 풀잎에 맺혔던 물방울들은 비가 그친 후 나온 햇살에 항복하듯이 바닥으로 떨어졌다. 토요일의 고요 속에서 마주한 성 조지 학교는 유럽의 나지막한 성을 연상시켰다. 축구장 두 배보다 더 넓은 잔디밭, 웅장한 건물과 오래된 담벼락에서 품격이 느껴졌다.

넓은 잔디밭은 텅 비어 있었으나 그 위에서 뛰어노는 소년들, 책을 읽는 모습, 장난과 웃음소리, 팔베개로 누워 하늘을 바라보는 모습, 나지막한 대화 등을 상상하며, 여고 시절로 돌아간 듯 한동안 서 있었다. 이렇게 아름답고 멋진 공간에서 학창 시절을 보내었다면 내 삶의 빛깔은 어떻게 달라졌을까. 그들은 책 속 지식뿐만이 아니라, 자연에서, 공간이 주는 품격과 여유도 배웠을 것이다.

I walked to the entrance of the forest remembering the road I went to in the morning. The water droplets on the grass fell to the ground as if surrendering to the sunlight that came out after the rain stopped. St. George's School, faced in the silence of Saturday, was reminiscent of a lowly castle in Europe. I felt dignity on the lawn, the magnificent building, and the old wall, which was more than twice the size of the soccer field.

The wide lawn was empty, but I stood for a while as if I had returned to my high school days, imagining boys running on it, reading books, jokes and laughter, lying on his arm pillow, looking up at the sky, and low-key conversations. If I had spent my school days in such a beautiful and wonderful space, how would the color of my life have changed? They must have learned not only the knowledge in the book, but also the dignity and relaxation that space gives in nature.

밴쿠버 대학 인류학 박물관

속이 안 좋을 때는 위장을 비우면서 죽처럼 부드러운 음식을 먹고, 배를 따뜻하게 하는 것이 빨리 회복하는 방법이었다. 집으로 돌아와, 한국서 가져간 누룽지를 삶아서 죽처럼 만들어 점심으로 먹었다. 다시 배를 따뜻하게 해주었다.

오후에 존이 밴쿠버대학 인류학 박물관에 차로 데려다주었다. 입구부터 뭔가 특별하였다. 입구에 우뚝 선 청동 조각 "The Knife" 앞에서 잠시 걸음을 멈추었다. 길게 뻗은 칼날과 원형의 디스크가 인간의 어깨와 하나로 이어진 모습이 친근하였다.

호모 파베르(Homo Faber), 도구를 쓰는 인간이라는 뜻처럼 인간이 도구와 함께 살아온 긴 역사를 압축하여 보여주는 것 같았다. 박물관 안 유물들이 과거의 흔적이 아니라 여전히 우리와 이어졌다고 은근히 암시하는 듯하였다.

UBC Museum of Anthropology

When I felt sick, the quick way to recover was to empty my stomach, ate soft food like porridge, and warm my stomach. When I returned home, I boiled the nurungji I took from Korea and made it like porridge for lunch. I warmed my stomach again.

I went to the Museum of Anthropology(MOA) in the afternoon by my host's car. From the the entrance, there was something special. I paused for a moment in front of the bronze statue "The Knife" standing tall at the entrance. It was friendly to see the elongated blade and circular disk connected to the human shoulder.

Like Homo Faber, a human using tools, it seemed to compress the long history of humans living with tools. It was secretly suggesting that the artifacts in the museum were still connected to us, not traces of the past.

넓고 높은 1층 공간에는 나무로 만들어진 거대한 캐나다 원주민 토템들이 관광객들을 맞이하듯 서 있었다. 우리나라 장승처럼 마을 표지를 알렸을 커다란 대문 조형물과 사람 모습의 조형물이 공간을 가득 채웠다. 수천 년의 세월을 견뎌온 나무 조각상 앞에 서니 여전히 그 시대 사람들의 노랫소리와 북소리가 들려오는 듯하였다.

인류학 5만 점, 고고학 535,000점, 여러 문화와 지역 유물 약 9천 점 등 인류학 박물관답게 전시품이 아주 많았다. 동서양의 도자기, 여러 나라의 탈과 오래전부터 사용했던 도끼, 칼, 창 등 원시적인 무기 등도 다양하였다. 나라마다 차이를 비교하는 재미가 쏠쏠하였다.

조명을 받은 진열장 안에 가득한 탈, 의식 도구, 도자기, 의류 등은 단순한 유물이 아니라 시대 모습을 보여주며 그들의 삶과 이야기와 정신을 고스란히 담고 있었다. 전시하지 못한 많은 유물이 아래쪽 서랍에 보관되어 있어서 교육 및 연구 자료로 충분하였다.

In the spacious and high ground floor space, huge native Canadian totems made of wood stood as if they were welcoming tourists. Like Jangseung in Korea, large gate sculptures that would have announced the village's cover and human-shaped sculptures filled the space. Standing in front of a wooden statue that has endured thousands of years, it still seemed that the songs and drums of the people of that era could be heard.

As an anthropology museum, there were many exhibits, including 50,000 anthropological items, 535,000 archaeological items, and about 9,000 cultural and local artifacts. There were also various ceramics from the East and the West, masks from various countries, and primitive weapons such as axes, knives, and spears that had been used for a long time. The fun of comparing differences between countries was also taken care of.

Masks, ritual tools, ceramics, and clothing filled with lights in the display case were not just artifacts, but showed the appearance of the times and contained the spirit and story of their lives. Many artifacts that were not displayed were stored in the lower drawers, so educational and research materials were sufficient.

심지어 한국에서도 보기 힘든 100년이 지난 아이 한복과 시집갈 때 사용한 요강까지. 별로 중요하지도 않은 하찮은 것까지 수많은 유물을 어떻게 모았을까. 누군가의 숨은 노력과 많은 경비와 오랜 시간이 걸렸을 텐데. 단순한 수집이 아니라 인류가 살아온 발자취를 고스란히 보여주고 있었다. 작은 그릇 하나에도 누군가의 손길과 삶의 무게가 담겨있다는 생각에 오랫동안 그곳에 머물며 그 시대를 상상하였다.

박물관 뒤쪽으로 나오니 해안선을 연상시키는 곡선미가 돋보이는 고요한 연못이 있었다. 물결 하나 없는 수면은 거울처럼 맑아, 연못 주변의 조형물과 자연들이 빠짐없이 반영되었다.

박물관 내부가 과거의 이야기를 들려주는 곳이라면, 연못은 그 모든 것을 고요히 안은 채 현재의 모습을 보여주는 평화스러운 곳이었다.

A 100-year-old children's Hanbok and the Korean chamber pot used to marry is hard see even in Korean normal museums. How did they collect so many artifacts that were not very important? It must have taken someone's hidden efforts, a lot of money, and a lot of time. It was not just a collection, but it showed the footsteps of mankind. Thinking that even a small bowl contained someone's touch and the weight of life, I stayed there for a long time and imagined the era.

When I came out of the back of the museum, there was a tranquil pond with a curved beauty reminiscent of the coastline. The water surface, without a wave was as clear as a mirror, reflecting the sculptures and nature surrounding the pond without a single flaw.

If the inside of the museum was a place to tell the story of the past, the pond was a peaceful place to show the present, holding it all still.

나의 몸 상태가 오전보다 훨씬 나아졌다. 저녁은 어제 재어둔 불고기와 잡채로 우리가 요리하였다. 존은 먹지 않는 채소가 많아서 고기에 버섯만 넣어서 따로 요리하였다. 모니카의 친구 마리(Mary)도 오셨고, 나나이모 섬에서 집에 다니러 온 큰딸도 함께 먹었다. 깜박 잊고 작은딸을 초대하지 못한 것이 미안했다.

큰딸은 종종 한국 음식을 먹은 경험이 있어서, 먹는 방법에 익숙하였다. 존 역시 스테이크보다 부드럽고, 짭조름하면서 달달한 불고기 양념 맛에 흡족해하였다. 마리는 한국 음식이 처음이라면서도 맛있게 드셨다. 밥은 한국 쌀이 없어서 맛없는 동남아산으로 지었으나 김에 싸서 먹으니 괜찮았다. 후식으로 아이스크림과 캐나다인이 즐긴다는 대황을 넣은 파이를 먹었는데 오묘한 향이 입속에 맴돌았다.

음식만으로도 한국의 문화와 캐나다 문화의 차이점을 알고, 서로 이해할 수 있으니 이 또한 민간외교가 아닌가?

My physical condition was much better than in the morning. We cooked dinner with measured bulgogi yesterday and japchae. For John, who has a lot of vegetables that he doesn't eat, I cooked separately by mixing only mushrooms with meat. Monica's friend Mary, who lives in the neighborgood, and their youngest daughter, who came home from Nanaimo on Vancouver Island, ate with us. I was sorry that I forgot to invite their eldest daughter.

Their youngest daughter often had the experience of eating Korean food, so she was familiar with how to eat it. John was also satisfied with the tender, salty, and sweet bulgogi seasoning on steak. Mari enjoyed Korean food even though it was her first time. Rice was made from Southeast Asia, which was not tasty because there was no Korean rice, but it was okay to eat it wrapped in seaweed. I had dessert ice cream and a rhubarb pie, a Canadian favorite, and a mysterious aroma lingered in my mouth.

Isn't this also private diplomacy because through food we can know and understand some of the difference between Korean and Canadian culture?

린 캐니언 공원, 캐필라노 리버 댐, 사이프레스 공원

밴쿠버는 세 번째 방문이다. 관광객이라면 한 번쯤 가는 곳이 캐필라노 현수교와 밴쿠버대학 안에 있는 누드 비치인데 나는 두 곳을 올 때마다 방문하였다. 차를 빌려 두 곳과 동계올림픽이 열린 휘슬러까지 다녀오려고 했는데 존이 마지막 날 원데이 호스트도 해준다고 하여 그를 믿었다.

존은 밴쿠버대학에서 암 역학과 생물통계학을 가르치다 퇴직하셨다. 그는 사이클링과 하루 두 끼 식사로 건강을 챙겼다. 또 그는 저소득층 노인들을 돕고, 암환자를 위한 운전과 푸드 뱅크에서도 봉사하고 있다. 간간이 머무는 서바스 회원에게 밴쿠버 소개를 즐기고 있었다.

퇴직 후에도 어딘가에서 자리를 차지하거나 돈을 벌려는 우리나라 고위직 은퇴자들이 욕심내지 않고 자신보다 못한 이들을 위해 봉사하고, 사회 활동에 앞서면 좋겠다. 봉사하는 습관을 기르기 위해 어릴 때부터 가정과 학교, 사회에서 가르치고, 어른들이 먼저 모범을 보여야 할 부분이다.

Lynn Canyon Park, Capilano River Dam, Cypress Park

It is my third visit to Vancouver. The Capilano Suspension Bridge and the University of Vancouver's Nude Beach are all tourist destinations, which I visited every time I visited them. I am going to rent a car and go to two places and Whistler, where the Winter Olympics were held, but did not because John said he would host one-day on the last day.

John retired from teaching Cancer Epidemiology and Biostatistics at the University of British Columbia. He was taking care of his health by cycling and eating only two meals a day. He helps the elderly in low-income families, drives for cancer patients, and volunteers at food banks. He also enjoys introducing Vancouver to the occasional Servas members.

Shouldn't Korea's high-ranking retirees who want to take a position or make money even after retirement be emulated? We should teach and set an example in the family, school, and society from an early age.

그가 우리를 데려간 세 곳은 관광객이 잘 가지 않는 현지인이 즐겨 찾는 곳이라 우리도 밴쿠버 시민이 된 듯 신이 났다. 지리를 잘 아는 존이 첫 번째로 우리를 데려간 곳은 노스밴쿠버에 있는 린 캐니언 공원이었다.

비싼 입장료를 내는 캐필라노 현수교는 관광 명소답게 잘 가꿔진 정원과 기념품 가게가 사람들을 맞이했던 기억이 있는데, 이곳은 입장료도 없고, 소박한 안내문과 숲 자체가 먼저 말을 걸어오는 듯하였다. 137m 길이를 가진 캐필라노 현수교는 출렁거려서 고소공포증이 있는 사람들에게는 아찔한데, 약 50m 길이의 짧은 린 캐니언 현수교는 단숨에 건널 수 있었다. 두 개의 현수교 아래로 에메랄드색의 맑은 캐필라노 강물이 똑같이 흘렀다.

특히 린 캐니언 공원에는 여러 개의 작은 폭포들과 여름에는 수영할 수 있는 웅덩이들이 있었다. 숲은 올림픽 반도의 크레스켄트 트레킹 코스와 크게 다르지 않았다. 침엽수림은 하늘을 가렸고, 뻗어 나온 가지에는 이끼가 뒤덮여 자라고 있었다.

The three places he took us to are rarely visited by tourists but locals favorite places, so we were excited as if we had become Vancouver citizens. The first place John, who knows the road, took us was at Lynn Canyon Park in North Vancouver,

The Capilano Suspension Bridge, which pays a high entrance fee, has a well-established garden and souvenir shop as a tourist attraction. But there was no entrance fee, and the simple notice and the forest itself seemed to be talking to me first. The 137 meters Capilano Suspension Bridge is dizzying for people with acrophobia, but the short Lynn Canyon Suspension Bridge, which is about 50 meters long, was able to cross at once. The clear, emerald waters of the Capilano River flowed equality beneath the two suspension bridges.

Especially in Lynn Canyon Park, there were several small waterfalls and pools for swimming in the summer. Th forest was not much different from the Creskent trekking course on the Olympic Peninsula. Coniferous forests obscured the sky, and moss was growing on the outstretched branches.

산책 코스를 걸으니 약 한 시간이 걸렸다. 제주의 곶자왈을 걷는 것처럼 익숙하였다. 뿌리가 드러난 나무, 쓰러진 나무 비좁은 틈 사이로 뿌리를 내려 자라는 식물 등이 함께 숲을 이루고 있었다. 사람들은 자연을 덜 훼손하려고 울퉁불퉁 만들어진 숲길을 걸으며 힐링하였다. 개와 함께 산책 나온 주민들은 일상인 듯 여유롭게 숲을 즐겼고, 조깅 단체 그룹은 전혀 힘들지 않은 듯 오르막길을 달렸다.

캐필라노 현수교는 여행자를 위한 무대였다면, 린 공원은 동네 사람들이 아끼는 비밀스러운 숲속 놀이터요, 주민들의 안식처였다. 주차비는 우리가 내려고 하였으나 존이 이미 해결하여서 미안함과 고마움이 교차하였다.

It took about an hour to walk on the walking course. It felt as familiar as walking along Gotjawal in Jeju. The forest was made up of trees with exposed roots, fallen trees, and plants growing through the narrow gaps between them. People healed by walking through the rugged forest paths that were built to minimize damage to nature. Residents who walked with dogs enjoyed the forest leisurely as if it were a daily routine, and jogging group ran up the hill as if it was no trouble at all.

The Capilano Suspension Bridge was a stage for travelers, and Lynn Park was a secret forest playground cherished by local people and a resting place for residents. We were going to pay for the parking, but John had already solved it, so we were sorry and grateful.

다음으로 간 곳은 캐필라노 댐이었다. 넓은 주차장 주변에는 피보다 붉은 철쭉과 단아한 핑크 작약이 봄을 여전히 붙들고 있었다.

거울처럼 맑은 호수가 푸른빛으로 고요히 누워 있었고, 호수 위에는 노스쇼어 산맥의 능선이 늠름하게 병풍처럼 펼쳐졌다. 이를 지켜보는 하얀 구름이 더해져 댐은 멋진 풍경화가 되었다. 옆으로 조금 걸어 댐 앞에 서니 자연과 인간의 힘이 서로 맞닿은 경계에 서 있는 듯하였다. 강을 막아 세운 콘크리트 벽 아래로 무섭게 쏟아지는 물이 협곡을 따라 은빛 강줄기를 만들고 있었다.

도시의 식수로 쓰이는 댐 내부는 접근이 제한되어 있어 호수는 더욱 신비로웠다. 댐 주변을 둘러싸고 있는 자연은 고요함 속에서 스스로 질서를 지키며 존재하고 있었다. 댐과 호수는 시민들의 생명수가 되고, 수백 년의 세월을 지켜온 숲은 여행자의 마음을 다독여 주었다. 인간이 자연을 지배하는 것이 아니라 자연의 품에 기대어 살아간다는 사실을 다시 깨달았다.

The next stop was the Capilano Dam. Red royal azaleas and elegant pink peonies still held on to spring around the spacious park.

The lake, which was as clear as a mirror, lay still in blue, and the ridges of the North Shore Mountains spread out like folding screens on the lake. The dam became a wonderful landscape with the white clouds watching it. As I walked a little to the side and stood in front of the dam, it seemed to be at the boundary where nature and human power met each other. The river was blocked by a concrete wall, and a stream of silver rivers was created along the gorge by the terrifying water pouring down it.

The lake, where access was restricted because it was used as drinking water for citizens, was more mysterious. The nature surrounding the dam, existed in silence, keeping order on its own. Dam and lake became the lifeblood of citizens, and the forest that had preserved hundreds of years comforted travelers. I realized again that humans do not dominate nature, but live in its arms.

마지막으로 간 곳은 사이프레스 공원이었다. 먼저 간 두 곳과 다르게 웨스트밴쿠버에 위치한 이곳은 한참 산 위로 올랐다. 1975년에 조성된 공원은 안내판이 보여주는 것처럼 여름에는 트레일 코스로, 겨울에는 스키나 스노보드 등으로 캐나다인들이 즐겨 찾는 곳이다. 호수와 습지도 있고, 숲에서 야생 동물도 볼 수 있으며, 캠핑 장소로도 좋은 곳이다.

빽빽한 삼나무 숲길을 따라 자동차는 단숨에 올라왔다. 전망대에서 우리는 밴쿠버 경관을 보는 것에 만족하였다. 먼 바다를 배경으로 빼곡하게 들어선 빌딩들이 안개 속에서 흐릿하게 보였다.

아래쪽에는 도심의 분주함이 자리하지만, 이곳에는 바람 소리와 새소리가 나의 귀를 채웠다. 발아래 세상은 빠르게 흐르지만, 이 산에서는 천천히, 여유롭게 시간이 흘러가는 듯하였다.

The last place we went was Cypress Park. Unlike the two places that went first, this place in West Vancouver climbed a long way up the mountain. The park, which was built in 1975, is a favorite destination for Canadians, such as a trail course in summer and skiing or snowboarding in winter, as the information board shows. There are lakes and wetlands, wild animals can be seen in the forest, and it is also a good place for camping.

Along the dense redwood forest path, the car came up at once. From the observation deck, we were satisfied with the view of Vancouver. Buildings packed against the background of the distant sea were blurred in the fog.

Down below is the busyness of the city center, but the sound of wind and birds filled my ears. The world flowed quickly underfoot, but time seemed to pass slowly and leisurely on this mountain.

스탠리 공원에서 자전거 모험

집으로 돌아오는 길에 존과 함께 스탠리 공원에 들렀다. 라이온스 게이트 다리가 잘 보이는 곳에 우리를 안내해 주었다. 스탠리 공원 역시 내가 밴쿠버에 올 때마다 들렀던 곳이다. 처음에는 걷고, 두 번째는 혼자 자전거로 다녔다. 존은 우리를 자전거 대여점 앞에 내려주고 집으로 갔다.

스탠리 공원에서의 자전거 여행은 작은 모험과 같았다. 혼자는 잘 타는데, 2인용은 처음이었다. 앞자리를 맡아야 했던 나는 무거운 쇳덩이를 끌어내듯 출발이 수월하지 않았다.

해안가에 만들어진 길은 좁고 구불구불하였고, 군데군데 막힌 구간 때문에 내렸다가 다시 출발해야 했다. 후배는 자전거 경험이 적어서 출발 때 균형을 맞추지 못했고, 자전거와 우리 둘의 몸무게는 온전히 나의 다리에 실렸다. 출발이 능숙하지 못해서 자꾸 쇠붙이와 부딪히니 부드러운 나의 허벅지는 온통 멍으로 물들었다.

Bike Adventure at Stanley Park

On the way home, we stopped by Stanley Park. He took us to a place with a good view of the Lions Gate Bridge. Stanley Park is also the place I visited every time I came to Vancouver. First, I walked and second, I cycled alone. John dropped us off in front of the bike rental store and went home.

The bicycle trip at Stanley Park was like a small adventure. I can ride well alone, but it was my first time for two. I had to take the front seat, but it was not easy to start like pulling a heavy metal ball.

The road along the coast was narrow and meandering, and because of the clogged sections, I had to get off and start again. My junior had little bicycle experience, so she couldn't balance it when I started, and the bicycle and the weight of the two of us were fully loaded on my legs. My soft thighs were all bruised as I kept bumping into the metal because I wasn't good at starting.

자전거 바퀴가 나감에 따라 풍경도 조금씩 달라졌다. 크기를 알 수 없는 크루즈 배는 잔잔하게 파도를 흔들며 그 자리를 지켰다. 어디를 향하는지 알 수 없는 화물선이 라이온스 게이트 다리 아래로 미끄러지듯 나아갔다. 거대한 철골의 다리 아래에서 나는 보잘것없는 자전거 위의 여행자였지만, 그 풍경 속에 함께 녹아든 순간만큼은 우주와 연결된 자유로운 영혼이었다.

분수 놀이터에 다다르자 아빠 품에 안긴 아가는 처음으로 마주하는 분수를 신기한 듯 바라보았다. 모래 해변에서는 젊은이들이 모래 위에 누워 일광욕을 즐기고 있었다. 숲 놀이터에서는 함께 나온 가족들의 웃음이 넘쳐났다.

힘든 페달질을 하는 길 위에서 흘러가는 수많은 이야기를 듣고, 있는 그대로의 자연을 만끽하였다. 고단함 속에서 아름다움과 즐거움을 발견하는 일은 여행이 주는 또 다른 선물이지 싶다.

As our cycling improved, the scenery changed little by little. The cruise ship, of unknown size, was standing by gently moving waves. A cargo ship with unknown destination glided under the Lions Gate Bridge. Under the huge steel-framed bridge, I was a humble traveler on a bicycle, but for the moment I melted into the landscape, I was a free spirit connected to the universe.

We approached the fountain playground, the baby in her father's arms looked at the fountain facing first time with wonder. On the sand beach, young people were lying on the sand and enjoying the sunbathing. The forest playground was full of laughter from the family who came out together.

I listened to numerous stories flowing on the road where I was pedaling hard, and enjoyed nature as it was. Finding beauty and joy in the midst of hardships is another gift from travel.

집으로 돌아와서 모니카가 해준 마지막 저녁을 먹었다. 그녀의 친구 마리와 다른 곳에 사는 그녀의 아들도 함께하였다. 저녁 메뉴 스파게티는 다른 재료가 든 것처럼 다른 맛과 정성이 느껴져서 더 맛있었다. 여럿이 밥을 먹으니 어릴 때 많은 식구가 모여 먹었던 기억이 떠올랐다. 부모님은 아이들 여럿을 키우려면 힘들겠지만 역시 자식은 여러 명이면 좋겠다.

밤에 오로라를 볼 수 있다는 소식을 듣고, 우리는 모니카를 따라서 집에서 멀지 않은 한적한 바닷가로 갔다. 우리처럼 오로라를 기다리는 몇 사람들이 보였다. 밤 10시가 되어도 오로라는 나타날 기미조차 보이지 않았다. 잠이 쏟아지는 모니카가 먼저 자리를 떴고, 우리는 더 기다렸지만 끝내 오로라는 모습을 보여주지 않았다. 특별한 마지막 밤을 기대했는데 아쉬웠다.

사람을 만나고, 밀밭을 찍기 위해 시작한 여행은 폭넓게 자연을 대하는 시각을 가지게 되었다. 모든 인간이 자연에 기대며, 자연과 함께 살고 있음을 진정으로 느꼈다. 자연 앞에서 왜 겸손해지는지 깨친 여행이었다.

처음 만난 낯선 이의 집에 머물렀지만 서바스 회원 댁은 전혀 낯설지 않았다. 친구나 친척 집에 온 것처럼 편하게 지냈다. 서로에 대한 정보를 조금이나마 알고, 다양한 방법으로 미리 연락하였기 때문이다.

세계 곳곳에 친구를 가진 나는 정말 사람 부자이다. 세계 평화구현의 취지에 동조하는 많은 사람이 관심을 가지고 함께 활동하기를 기대한다.

When I came back home, I had the last dinner Monica made for me. Her friend Mary and her son, live in another place, also joined. The spaghetti on the dinner menu was even more delicious because it had a different flavor and was made with different ingredients. Eating together reminded me of the memory of having a large family when I was young. Parents must have a hard time raising many children, but I hope there are many family members.

We heard that we could see the aurora(Northen Lights) that night. We followed Monica to quiet beach not far from home. We could see some people waiting for the aurora like us. The aurora didn't even appear at 10 o'clock. Monica, who was full of sleep, left first. We waited longer, but the aurora never showed up. I was looking forward to a special last night, but it was disappointing.

The journey I started to meet people and to take picture of the wheat field gave me a broad perspective on nature. I truly felt that all humans leaned on nature and lived with it. It was a journey that reminded me of why I was humbled in front of nature.

Although I was staying in the house of a stranger I had just met, the Servas member's house didn't feel unfamiliar at all. I felt comfortable, as if I were staying at a friend's or relative's home. Because we knew a little bit about each other and had contacted each other in advance through various methods.

I am truly a rich person, having friends all over the world. I hope that many people who agree with the purpose of achieving world peace will take interest and participate in activities together.